RECONSTRUCTING HAPPY

How to Use Your Divorce as an
Opportunity to Build a Better You

Heather Tannenbaum

RECONSTRUCTING HAPPY
HOW TO USE YOUR DIVORCE AS AN
OPPORTUNITY TO BUILD A BETTER YOU

iUniverse books may be ordered through booksellers or by contacting:

iUniverse
1663 Liberty Drive
Bloomington, IN 47403
www.iuniverse.com
1-800-Authors (1-800-288-4677)

Because of the dynamic nature of the Internet, any web addresses or links contained in this book may have changed since publication and may no longer be valid. The views expressed in this work are solely those of the author and do not necessarily reflect the views of the publisher, and the publisher hereby disclaims any responsibility for them.

Any people depicted in stock imagery provided by Getty Images are models, and such images are being used for illustrative purposes only.
Certain stock imagery © Getty Images.

ISBN: 978-1-5320-5544-7 (sc)
ISBN: 978-1-5320-5543-0 (e)

Library of Congress Control Number: 2018911233

Print information available on the last page.

iUniverse rev. date: 10/08/2018

Contents

Welcome To Your New Life; An Introduction vii

About The Book ix

How to Use This Book xi

3 Basic Points About Divorce xiii

Part 1: My Story

Chapter 1:   The Ugliness of Labels; the Uniqueness of Tattoos............1

Chapter 2:   The Early Days and Mending Myself 3

Chapter 3:   You're Getting Divorced. Word Travels Fast....................7

Chapter 4:   My End-of-Marriage 'To Do' List.................................14

Chapter 5:   Logic Sleeps At Night...Panic Doesn't........................... 18

Chapter 6:   Bad Days; The Ugly Emotions.................................... 20

Chapter 7:   Significant OTHERS (as in, other than you)................... 25

Chapter 8:   Divorce Sucks. Life Doesn't. 28

Part 2: Kids and Co-Parenting

Chapter 9:   Telling the Kids.. 33

Chapter 10: Kids... 36

Chapter 11: Divorce Pains vs. Growing Pains;
            Understanding My Kids 39

Chapter 12: The "Co" in Co-Parenting means Cooperative...
            Not Competitive! 43

Chapter 13: How to Act Right When Your Ex Acts Wrong................. 52

Part 3: Friendship

Chapter 14: Friends 59

Chapter 15: Being a Good Friend 62

Chapter 16: Mutual Friends.. 64

Part 4: Moving Forward and Rebuilding

Chapter 17: Reprogramming Yourself... 69
Chapter 18: A Theme Song.. 73
Chapter 19: Rebuilding Myself.. 75
Chapter 20: Meeting New People, Friends and Others......................... 77
Chapter 21: The Next Chapter.. 83

Part 5: The Business of Divorce

Advice from Family Law experts and Financial Professionals 87

Welcome To Your New Life;
An Introduction

"The first step towards getting somewhere is to decide you're not going to stay where you are."
— *John Piermont Morgan*

So you're getting divorced. Welcome. You're now an exclusive member of a club that you likely never saw yourself in, nor wanted to be a member of. Maybe you're freaking out. Maybe a part of you is relieved or even excited at the prospect. Your emotions are likely all over the place, as mine were; you're feeling a range of emotions, and your outlook switches from one minute to the next.

Ready or not, here we go...It's time to steer yourself through the unknown. Who will you be? What does this mean for your kids? What will your relationship with them look like in this new life? What kind of relationship will you have with your ex? Roles and rules are being re-defined. If you're reading this, then all these questions have likely occupied your thoughts and possibly robbed you of precious sleep and time.

In time, you'll be able to answer all of these uncertainties. You're in charge of your life and though it may not feel like it right now, you hold the answers to all that overwhelms you. YOU. Regardless of what type of passive or active role you took in your marriage or its destruction, this is a new time; a time of rebuilding; for you to take control of your life and re-define yourself. Who do you WANT to be? If you've got young children, they're depending on you, and you've got no choice but to depend on yourself. This is your chance to reconstruct your own happy.

Are you up for the task? I didn't think I was. I needed to figure out where I fit in, in this new life, and in these new roles. There are so many self-help books out there to assist you. Many of them are good. They're written mostly by professionals who can offer much insight and advice into what you need to do to be amicable with your ex, co-parent your children effectively and manage your finances. The experts will tell you that the dust tends to settle after the first 2 years of separation.

But to me, that seemed like an awfully long way away. I needed help now and didn't know where to start... I found helpful advice in the pages of some of these books, but it all felt a little too clinical for me. I wanted to hear from someone who had gone through it. I wanted to be able to relate to the author's stories and I didn't want to always feel like I was in therapy or being talked at. I just wanted to know how other regular, everyday people handled it. I also needed to gauge how I was doing relative to others. I didn't want to feel so isolated, and I needed validation.

And so, this book was born.

About The Book

"It's never too late to be who you might have been."
– George Eliot

I began writing this book exactly one year after I had separated from my husband of 14 years. One year: One of each season, birthday, holiday, and non-anniversary. In the 12 months leading up to this book, I had watched my children wear their label, "children of divorce"; A label that my husband and I at the time, shamefully and very reluctantly stuck on our children, as a result of our choices.

This book has undergone so many transformations and appearances in its development, but when it was finally born, it was everything I needed it to be. It was also written and re-written from a healthy place. Grief can be healthy and functional.

Why this book? That first year was a very lonely one in many ways for me. Regardless of the kind of support system you have in place, there are times that you're going to feel alone. This book is meant to be your private, unconditional, judgement-free outlet. My lonely times still happen on weekends when the house is clean and quiet or when the kids are spending a holiday or long weekend with their dad.

It's during your lonely times or just some quiet time that I want you to pick up this book. Read it. Pick a section that applies or randomly open to any page. I hope you laugh. I hope you cry. I hope you share your inner feelings and thoughts, whether it's on paper through the exercises provided, or just out loud in an empty room.

I didn't find any self-help books that I really connected with. I decided to build my own but not for publication. My intention rather, was to document my personal journey and gauge my progress. As I began writing however, I realized that I had actually grown over the past 12 months and that now I not only had perspective, but I had been there, done that, and come out better and stronger than ever. I reconstructed my own happy. With some encouragement from a few good friends, I decided to share my experience with others in the hopes that your first year would be a little less lonely and so that you could take my experiences along on your journey, relate to and learn from them, identify with them and make this book a part of your growth, healing and reconstruction. Writing this book was part of my healing. Reading it will hopefully be part of yours.

Why share my story and why should you care? It's quite simply the story of an everyday, somewhat average 40 year old who found her entire world changed through her divorce from a divorce lawyer. My goal with this book is to give you a well-balanced, well-rounded approach to coping, managing and rebuilding yourself. It's my story, infused with the advice of a health care professional and it's practical tips that you'll need for the legal and financial aspects of your divorce.

How to Use This Book

This is intended to be a 3-in-1 book. Throughout the book, you'll notice "Dr. J. Says" blurbs. These are valuable contributions by Dr. K.A. Jablonowski, who has worked as a psychiatrist and therapist for over 12 years and has had extensive experience counselling spouses and families going through separation and divorce. She provides expert advice throughout this book and offers helpful commentary throughout my story.

Dr. Jablonowski graduated with her M.D.C.M from McGill University and continued on at McGill university in Montreal to complete 5 years of specialized training in psychiatry. Dr. Jablonowski received the most promising psychiatrist award upon completion of her training and continued on to be a well respected and often consulted member of the psychiatric community in the greater Toronto region of Ontario. I am so grateful for her help and input on this project.

At the end of this book, there's a section on the business of divorce. As you begin to look for a lawyer and get into the legal aspect of your divorce, I wanted to provide you with some helpful tips and guidance for finding the right lawyer for you and how to use your lawyer efficiently and effectively. For this section, I relied not only on my personal experience, but you will find advice from several lawyers. While my book doesn't identify who they are, the advice provided is the combination of 2 lawyers who specialize in Family Law. There are also some helpful tips on how to manage your finances from financial experts. 2 of the experts are Canadian financial planners and one is an American Certified Divorce Financial Analyst, Shawn Leamon. I hope you find my journey helpful in yours.

At the beginning of each chapter, there's a quote that I feel is reflective of the chapter. They're either famous quotes or quotes by famous people. It's my hope that some of these quotes will resonate with you. Throughout the book there are also "Just For Fun" pieces as well as some exercises for you to do if you so choose. They're intended to be fun, reflective and interactive. However you opt to use this book, I thank you for putting some faith in me and for taking me along as you begin to build your new happily ever after.

3 Basic Points About Divorce

Let's get a few things straight at the onset:

1. Divorce Has Evolved. So Must Our Views.

> "It always seems impossible until it's done."
> *- Nelson Mandela*

Divorce today is viewed and managed very differently than it was decades ago. Today, we encourage co-parenting and we understand the detrimental effects of parental alienation. We understand now more than ever, that children's psychological well-being doesn't hinge upon whether their parents are married, but whether their parents can each provide stability, love and security. We no longer use terms like "broken home". My family was broken when we were married. We mended it through divorce. We now understand that divorce doesn't destroy children... high conflict holds the potential to, irrespective of marital status. Families today are so diverse, and where in the past this wasn't well understood or accepted, today we know that children can benefit from a loving environment, regardless of what the family unit looks like.

2. Your Journey Must Begin With Forgiving Yourself

> "Peace comes from within. Do not seek it without."
> *– Gautama Buddha*

Bad choices are inevitable in life. Going through a divorce or any life-altering event always stirs things up. They force you to look back at some of your choices and help you figure out how you got to where you are. I definitely made some bad choices, but it's not always that simple.

Looking back allows us some much needed distance and perspective to reflect upon our choices, but it can also cloud how we felt in the moment. With time comes distance. Perhaps we made bad choices but perhaps we also made the best choice we could in a bad situation, given the circumstances at the time. There's a difference between making a bad choice, and making a difficult choice in a bad situation.

There were other factors at play at the time, which have since escaped you. Once you're able to recognize this, then you're able to forgive yourself. Forgiving oneself is quintessential. Perspective is helpful, but forgiveness is necessary. You may not remember why, but believe in yourself, that you likely had good reason for your choice in that moment. We can't go back and change it. We can only look back and have trust in ourselves that although the outcome wasn't what we had hoped, it was the best that we could do at the time. Only then can you truly achieve forgiveness and closure.

> Dr. J. Says: Feeling guilt is a normal part of grieving a loss, and divorce is a significant loss. In the case of divorce, you're not only grieving the loss of a person but also of a way of life you had become comfortable with. Like feelings of sadness and anger, guilt is a normal emotional experience. Grieving takes time and like a rollercoaster, it has its ups and downs. If you feel the guilt is too much to handle on your own, talking to a professional can sometimes help you to stop blaming yourself.

3. Divorce Sucks...Let's Get Real. Let's Deal!

"When you break up, your whole identity is shattered.
That's why it's like death. It *is* a death."

– *Dennis Quaid*

"Wanting to be someone else is a waste of who you are"

– *Kurt Cobain*

When we go through a divorce, our life is indeed shattered; broken and smashed into many jagged and fragmented pieces. Every aspect of our life is affected. Work. Social. Family. Finances. Private issues now seem open for public consumption, and while I'm not Kim Kardashian, I felt kind of like I was. I obviously don't have a media frenzy circling my home, waiting to catch me living my life, but in my mind, it felt like there was. I felt like my very private life and my very private struggles were on display for everyone in my world. I didn't need to be on the cover of tabloids to feel exploited and exposed. I felt that way in my own world, in my own community, small as it may be in terms of audience, it felt very big to me.

Divorce sucks. Truly. Regardless of whether you initiated it, wanted it or fought like hell to avoid it, it always sucks! Who's ever prepared to pick up the pieces? It's the situation that we're in; how we got here doesn't matter. We owe it to our children and to ourselves to mend and move on.

We're all familiar with that defeated and deflated feeling when we've worked so hard building a Lego structure and it gets knocked down? Or when your computer crashes before you were able to save your brilliantly written paper? Worst feeling ever....But, once you re-build the structure or re-write the paper, you find that it's better than the original. Think of yourself as that Lego structure. We're not Humpty Dumpty...we don't simply want to put our pieces back together. This is your opportunity to reconstruct a better, stronger version of yourself. You get to pick and choose which pieces belong and which don't.

On my good days, I thought of my situation as my second chance. New dreams and new opportunities awaited. I knew this would require hard work, but my life could be rewarding and fulfilling in ways I never imagined. I just had to start.

Part One

My Story

CHAPTER 1

The Ugliness of Labels; the Uniqueness of Tattoos

"It ain't what they call you, it's what you answer to."
— *W.C. Fields*

"We repeat what we don't repair."
— *Christine Langley-Obaugh*

Just like those sticky name tags that I slap onto my kids' clothes and gear, I had now branded and burdened my children with a more permanent one, and not one that I could pretty up by adding butterflies or smiley emojis. No, this label was one that my children would have to learn how to wear and bear. And it was my job to teach them how. But how?? I was in uncharted waters, and the waters were rough. How could I possibly navigate them and myself towards a place of calm, when my heart and soul were in a turbulent upheaval? I too had to wear my new label but I wanted to put my issues aside and deal with 2 more immediate concerns; my kids, who needed guidance except that I had no idea how to do it.

My children were 7 and 9 when we told them that Mommy and Daddy feel that it's best for our family if we don't live together anymore. My kids' emotions were all over the place...Shock, Fear, Sadness, Anger and even Excitement at the prospect of a second home and a dog. They got the new home, but they had to wait quite a bit longer for the dog!

Life tried to label us. Let's turn that label into our tattoo. Our own unique and beautiful stamp on life!

Telling the kids about our divorce was quite possibly the most difficult and gut-wrenching experience of our lives. I say "our" because despite the fact that we are no longer a 'we', my Ex-husband is still the father of my children and he loves them as much as I do. He is the only other one who worried as I worried during pregnancy and birth. He is the only one who shared those early and fundamental milestones and experiences with me. Because our relationship broke along the way, does not negate his love for our children and to deny his role in their life would only disservice our kids. That in my opinion, is the first step in helping your children heal and subsequently, transform their label into a tattoo; CHOOSE THEM OVER ANYTHING ELSE, especially over your own broken heart or your feelings for your ex.

> Dr. J Says:
>
> Divorce, just like marriage is common. In Western cultures over 90% of people have married by age 50. Of this group 40-50% will experience a divorce. Given this high number most of us will be touched by this life changing experience in one way or another.[1]

---

[1] American Psychological Association

The Early Days and Mending Myself

"It's sad, something coming to an end. It cracks you open, in a way – cracks you open to feeling."

– Jennifer Aniston

"Definitions belong to definers, not the defined."

– Toni Morrison, Beloved

Above all, I felt like an epic failure. I had failed on every level of humanity. As a wife, as a woman, and as a mother. I was completely broken. I have always been a "half-full" kind of girl, but in the months following our decision to separate, I didn't even feel half-empty...I was a complete zero. Nothing in the tank. Numbness was the best feeling, and I longed for the days when sheer exhaustion from fear and heartbreak kicked in and I was too spent to feel a thing. It was far better than the alternative.

What did I fear? Almost everything. I was terrified of the implications of divorce on my children, on my finances and how my friends would treat me. How many friends would I lose in this process? Hadn't I lost enough? I couldn't deal with any further hurt or losing anyone or anything else. I was so deep into my sorrow that it clouded any perspective. Nothing in my life was settled. Nothing in my life was certain or known. I was damaged, broken and petrified of what our lives would look like when the dust settled, or if it ever would.

I had never experienced panic attacks until I separated. My stomach was in knots more often than not and by the end of the day, my stomach pains were so severe that I often couldn't even stand up straight. I was so hurt emotionally, that it physically took its toll. I was void and I was alone and I was scared. I was paralyzingly terrified for what lay ahead for me and my children.

I married a divorce lawyer when I was 25 and I divorced him the year of my 40th birthday. I had a promising career and then shifted all my focus to raising our daughter and then our son as well, 2 years later. I loved my life. I loved my family. I loved our home and our friends. I wasn't so naïve as to believe that this wouldn't change...I just desperately wanted to hang onto some type of stability and normalcy for me and my kids.

Emotions were never something that I was good at expressing. I have always shown warmth, love and affection towards my children but I was clueless when it came to expressing and identifying emotion. I had misattributed emotion for weakness. I never cried, and I truly believed that that's what defined my strength. When I began this journey, I didn't even know that about myself. Through much self-reflection, several good friends, therapy and a lot of painful retrospection, I have been able to tap into my emotions and begin to feel. It feels good to feel...I had lost that ability somewhere along the way. I have cried more in the past 12 months than in the 12 years prior. Not all sadness....just emotions. Pure, raw emotion.

My kids will now roll their eyes and say "oh no, Mommy's being emotional again", to which I reply, "What's wrong with that? It's just my way of showing my feelings and it takes a strong person to show that". I own my feelings and I wear them proudly: Another step in transforming and in re-constructing myself.

Dr. J. Says:

There is a misconception out there that expressing emotions is "weak". That if you are coping well your emotions should be in control. Truthfully emotions are important for normal psychological function. If you are sad and angry and try to keep that in you may end up doing more harm than good. Evidence shows people who tend not to express emotions have a higher risk of health conditions such as high blood pressure and substance abuse. Feelings are normal and should be expressed. If that is difficult for you with family and friends, a therapist or support group may be a safer alternative where you feel ready to express emotion without being judged.

Labels are pre-conceived notions and opinions of who we are and what defines us. Labels are other people's ideas of us. We can choose to wear them in shame and allow all future self-opinions to be ruled by this label affixed to us, but we have another option. A better, liberating, happier option.

We can transform our label into a tattoo. I am referring specifically to the modern, North American tattoo which is done with artistic intent and done voluntarily. The type of tattoos to which I refer, are body art that people willingly and proudly acquire and wear with pride. It is something to be admired and enjoyed by self and others. It doesn't define us, but it becomes part of us; a beautiful part. It enhances us. Why can't labels become tattoos? Why can't we transform our labels into tattoos? WE CAN!

I'm divorced...so what? While I may not accept a label affixed to me, it's still there. It's always there. How I choose to look at it is up to me. How I teach my children to wear their label is up to me but how they eventually choose to wear it is up to them, and based entirely on the tools that I provide to them now.

So how does one go from a state of completely broken to a state of acceptance? How do I begin to re-build myself? It's an arduous journey but a necessary and rewarding one.

You're Getting Divorced. Word Travels Fast....

"Rumor travels faster, but don't stay put as long as truth."
— *Will Rogers*

"Strong minds discuss ideas, average minds discuss events, weak minds discuss people."
— *Socrates*

The breakdown and eventual break-up of my marriage was a huge loss; A devastating and tragic loss and as such, there is a natural mourning period. When someone dies, there are religious and social customs and traditions that are adhered to. While divorce is certainly no longer a new phenomenon, there is no set of standards or customs to follow. This led me into the unknown. I went about my day to day responsibilities but everything was a struggle. My routine trip to Walmart suddenly became stressful for me. I was anxious about any potential social situation. I didn't want to be around people. I wasn't clinically depressed, I knew that I didn't require medication, but I was sad and embarrassed and I felt as though I was being judged; I probably was. I wore my label but I lacked the tools at this point to accept it.

I dreaded bumping into someone that I knew. Even the simplest question, "How are you?" was stressful and I was unsure how to answer it. I worried about whether they knew or whether I should tell them. How do I tell them? What are they thinking? I made an extra effort to dress nicely and make myself presentable. If I was put together on the outside, then surely they would think my heart and mind matched. I quickly adopted a "fake it til I make it" mentality.

Other people's opinions of me had always been inconsequential before, but now, post separation, it was all new. I was feeling something that I hadn't felt, or hadn't known I had felt since those awkward teenage years….insecurity. And everything I did was motivated by my desire to look strong and happy to those around me, including, and embarassingly, my ex-husband.

The subject of divorce makes people uncomfortable. It seems that we all know someone who is divorced, but I learned that it actually makes people uncomfortable. They feel that they have to choose sides and they don't know what to say or how to act. People are curious and while some have the gumption to ask specifics, most will simply discuss it with their friends in the form of gossip.

Gossip seems to be a constant yet unfortunate characteristic of human existence. Nothing feeds the "grapevine" more than tragedy and I was not immune. The "grapevine" was quick to snatch my news and begin churning out theories, speculations and inevitably, rumors; some comical, some cruel.

Gossip is so cruel because it's manufactured and perpetuated by people. No one is ever in a position to judge yet there they are, hearts closed, mouths open, eagerly awaiting the distribution rights to the "grapevine's" finished product, and taking creative liberties along the way.

Dr. J. Says:

In today's world of social media and instant communication gossip has become a pervasive problem. Not only can gossip spread faster than ever but your children may become privy to private facts about your impending divorce. The reasons to spread rumors can be numerous. Generally people tend not to see gossip as harmful to the person being discussed though it often can be devastating. If you are in the position where you become aware of gossip about yourself or spouse it is important to remember that it will quickly pass. Your life is more interesting to you than others and people will soon be on to the next story. If it is a friend spreading the rumors confronting them in a calm manner and explaining the hurt they may be doing to you and your children is usually a step in the right direction.

Exercise:

Here are some adjectives provided to me when I took to social media and asked my friends to describe 'gossip'.

Gossip Is:

Cruel	*Ugly*	*Toxic*	*Non-retractable*
Destructive	*Mean*	*Damaging*	*Negative*
Unproductive	*Wasteful*	*Petty*	*Reserved for the weak*

Write down a list of how gossip makes you feel and beside it, list how you can overcome these feelings:

How Gossip Makes Me Feel   *How Can I Overcome It*

_____   _____

_____   _____

_____   _____

_____   _____

Notice a theme? What do you notice:

So if so many people are obviously aware of the negative effects, then why do they do it? Here is mine: Inevitable.

Feel free to add your own:

Just For Fun:

Make up a rumor about yourself. Make it juicy and so off the charts. Write it down here, almost like a short story. Completely fake! I found this to be a silly but fun exercise. At the peak of gossip, I found that doing this helped me put into perspective just how ridiculous gossip is and it helped me laugh at myself and subsequently, laugh it off a bit.

I needed to simply catch my breath and in those early months, this was very difficult. Things moved very quickly for me and it seemed as though everything around me was happening in triple time but I was stuck in slow motion. When my husband and some of my furniture moved out, the carpet had indentations, highlighting where furniture used to reside. There it was, out there in the open, exposed. I desperately wanted to cover up the unsightly markings with new furniture. The thing is...you can't just cover up a wound or an indentation, and pretend it isn't there. No amount of hiding it or covering it up would change the fact that my carpet was damaged. I realized too, one night as I sat with a glass of wine, staring at the carpet, that while it was no longer pristine, it was fine. It had gone through regular wear and tear, just as I was going through. I began to cry. A lot. I was crying not only from sadness but because I could finally begin to accept the fact that I was no longer pristine. I carried scuff marks and indentations and general wear and tear. I wasn't broken. I was scared and wounded. I was labelled. And I would be ok.

> Dr. J. Says: The classic model for grief was first developed by Elisabeth Kubler Ross. Her 5 stage model for grief is useful in understanding what is going on inside you as you mourn the loss of your marriage. The five stages are denial, anger, bargaining, depression and acceptance. Where you are in that cycle can change as time goes on. You may get stuck at one stage or move back and forth between 2 stages for longer than you anticipated. There is no right and wrong in grieving the loss of your marriage and everyone is different so don't compare.[2]

Just for fun....

KIDS MAY SAY THE FUNNIEST THINGS, BUT ADULTS...WELL, HERE'S WHAT THEY SAY! Just for fun, here are some phrases that people often say in an attempt to lift spirits and inspire. They don't often have the desired effect, but if we understand why people say them, we can hear them with more appreciation and less anger:

---

[2] the Grief Cycle model first published in On Death & Dying, Elisabeth Kübler-Ross, 1969.

"It wasn't meant to be"

"Stay positive"

"You'll be fine"

"You're so pretty. You'll find someone else"

"You need to stay strong"

"You're so strong and brave. You'll get through this"

"I don't know how you get out of bed everyday"

"I know how you feel. My friend's mom got divorced"

"It'll be great. It was for the best"

"You're so lucky that you get to be a part-time mom"

"I wish I got time off like you do"

"You get the best of both worlds" (no, not a Miley Cyrus quote)

"At least you don't have a man to answer to" (yes, this was actually said to me)

Add your own here:

It all comes down to the fact that people don't know what to say, but they feel compelled to say something when quite often, a wordless hug or smile would be much more appreciated. Because I was in such an emotional state, I found it very difficult to hear their attempted words of encouragement. Instead of hearing their whispering undertones of good intentions, I only heard the scream of their words. Now when I hear such comments, I try to keep it in perspective and take them for exactly what they are, someone's support, albeit, misguided.

Dr. J. Says:

Sigmund Freud once told us that "anger turned inward is depression". Anger is a normal emotion we all experience. How we deal with that anger goes a long way in determining how we will cope with difficult life experiences. Anger at people around you can make you feel helpless. Helpless feelings can lead to sadness and even depression. If you find you can't get past the anger getting help to do so is a great idea. In the meantime if you can't calmly express the anger you feel towards the right person writing a letter to them or writing in a journal is often a great substitute. As you right and read back your words you may discover you are able to let the negative feelings go.[3]

---

[3] Sigmund Frued On Mourning and Melancholia (need reference)

CHAPTER 4

My End-of-Marriage 'To Do" List

"Grief is in two parts. The first is loss. The second is the remaking of life."

- Anne Roiphe

I found that when my husband moved out, I needed desperately to try new things. Everything around me seemed different now, and therefore I was determined to try to adapt. I wanted to embrace change. As someone who typically resists change, this was another large step, but all part of my process. I figured that if I embraced and accepted change, then the outcome would have to be favorable. I was making small and arbitrary changes, but on the whole, I was simply surviving the only way I could. My life was changing so I needed to change too. I tried new foods, I changed the brand of coffee I drank, I found a new hair stylist, and I tried to change the way I dressed.

I was trying to get to know myself again. Getting to know a new me and reconstructing who I wanted to be. I didn't know at the time that this is what I was doing, but it became clearer to me as time passed. Some of the changes stuck, some didn't, but I changed.

One of the more significant things I did, was I went to see a psychic. I had never really had an opinion about psychics one way or another, but all of a sudden I felt an urge to go.

It was strange and certainly different. All she knew was my first name. I didn't throw too much faith her way, but as soon as I sat down, she could tell I was nervous. This I attribute not to her psychic powers, but rather to my obvious body language.

The first thing she said to me? Are you married? I said "yes". She then told me that I was on a rocky path and that I was about to come out of a real darkness.

She went on of course, about many things. Some accurate, some lucky guesses perhaps, based on other inferences that I had revealed during our session. But I got what I had come for.

I'm not recommending that a psychic is the answer to our problems and that we're changed people once we leave our reading, but for me it was therapeutic. A psychic may not be the answer for you, and it wasn't really an answer for me, but I wasn't looking for answers. I wanted to try something new, keep an open mind and I wanted to feel that I was ok; That my choices have been good. I suppose I was seeking validation.

Find whatever tools you need, and utilize them. Whether it's a psychic, a friend, a good book, whatever your tool of choice, use it.

Dr. J. Says: Everyone copes differently. A good place to start is on the internet looking up resources for those going through a divorce. Maybe that is how you came upon this book. Self-help books and support groups can be great at helping you feel less alone. If you find you are using unhealthy ways to cope such as using substances, over or under eating or avoiding people or things it is worth considering trying something new. Replace a bad habit with a good one and see how it changes your outlook. Instead of avoiding people, call a friend. Instead of sleeping too much go to the gym. If the problems feel beyond control or out of control seek professional help.

Advice to Follow or Not…

Try new foods

Try new places…restaurants, or other venues you like, but change it up. Break old routines

Exercise. If you don't work out, try it. If you do work out, try a different type. If you're all about the cardio, try yoga. If you're all about the Zen, try kick boxing. Just change it up. Keep an open mind. Lots of things are changing that you don't have control over. Make some changes that are within your scope of control. You may actually discover some new things about yourself.

Change your bedroom. If you're moving to a new home, this is a given, but try not to mirror your last bedroom. If you're staying in your home, change it up a bit. This doesn't have to be costly, and shouldn't since your financial situation is likely precarious at best, you want to be wise with your spending. More on this in the final section of the book. Paint the room yourself. It gives you a project to do when the kids are with their other parent, and it'll freshen up the room. Add some new accessories; pillows, blanket, a new piece of art (I framed some of my kids' artwork and hung it in my room). Simply make a few changes to your room to reflect YOUR taste. You're no longer sharing your room. Make it yours.

Jewellery. Unless you're really financially strapped, I would suggest not selling jewelry or anything from your ex for at least a year. Put it away and in a year, you can decide what to do with it. You may wish to sell certain pieces (I waited a year and then sold my wedding band and engagement ring). To avoid making an emotional decision that you may regret, let time pass and feelings settle.

Parent your kids as if you're still married. They shouldn't have wiggle room to manipulate and play one parent off the other. Easier said than done, I know. More on this later.

Meet new people. I'm not referring to people who are in a similar situation necessarily, or even people you want to date. Just new people. Male, female, old, young, energetic, somber, whatever.

Be open and you'll be amazed at the interesting people you'll encounter.

I chose to look at myself like a butterfly, just fresh from my cocoon. It sounds very cliché, I know, but it was helpful for me to look at things like this. I was the same soul that I had always been, and the world was the same as it had always been. What was different however, was how I could fit into this world and what role I wanted to play. Meeting new people, trying new things really helped me to not only re-discover myself, but put me on the right track to reconstructing my happiness.

CHAPTER
5

Logic Sleeps At Night... Panic Doesn't

"Divorce is something that I never dreamed would happen to me. But it did."

- Dick Van Dyke

Once evening comes and the kids are tucked in for the night, I have a chance to breathe and reflect. I reflect on my day. Did I have a "good Mommy" day? Was I the kind of Mom today that I strive to be? Did I lose my patience? Was I an attentive listener; an effective problem solver? Did I give my kids what they needed today? I have always re-lived my day in my mind once my kids are asleep, but now, I had nobody to share this with and I had nobody to tell me that I was being too hard on myself. I needed to be my own cheerleader and my own analyst. I needed to hold it together during the day for my kids, and put my own pieces together at night...for myself.

And now I had thrown in another ingredient...a heaping portion of worry about my children's future. What would it look like? Would I be able to give them the life they have grown accustomed to? Would they grow up resentful that vacations stopped? Would vacations stop? I had no idea. Would they be capable of a healthy relationship or was I setting a poor example?

My panic attacks in the early months were a regular part of my nights. They've tapered off with time and as I began to have more faith in myself and my independence. Once things began to be real instead of just "what ifs", my panic attacks subsided.

Every once in a while, I'm caught off guard by a panic attack, and I'm hopeful that as time goes by, they'll become a part of my past. I am learning how to overcome them faster and they're not quite as intense as they used to be. I'm still holding out hope that more time will be the cure I need.

Dr. J Says: A panic attack is a symptom of anxiety characterized by sudden onset of physical feelings of anxiety such as racing heart, sweating, chest pains, trouble breathing and for some even fainting. Not everyone experiences panic attacks but for those who do the first thought is often that they are having a heart attack or other medical condition. Once you make sure it is indeed a panic attack, the next step involves educating yourself about what they are and how to manage them. Deep breathing, meditation and other relaxation techniques are very helpful with this kind of symptom. Over time the panic attacks should get less and less frequent.

CHAPTER 6

Bad Days; The Ugly Emotions

"Divorce is the most difficult thing you could ever go through in your entire life."

– Bethenny Frankel

Everyone is entitled to a bad day now and then, but sometimes during this process (and still today) it feels like my bad days are really bad. I gave so many years completely to being a mom and it was a 24/7 job. It isn't glamourous. It isn't always fun, but it's always important and it meant that I was always needed. I always had purpose. My presence always mattered. I was relevant. I was there. I was Mommy.

Once my husband moved out, everything changed. My world was shaken. My kids were ok. They saw Mommy and Daddy getting along. We presented a united front for the kids, regardless of whatever personal turmoil I was struggling through. Thankfully we were able to keep our kids somewhat immune and protected.

When they would go to Daddy's house on Tuesday nights, I was a misery. My house was clean, quiet and empty. I had loads of time to catch up on housework, school forms and whatever else I never seemed to get around to when the kids were around. It was empty.

My unhealthy thinking went something like this: What gave their dad the right to take them away from me? I'm their mother, and a pretty good one. I know he has legal rights, and I know that my kids benefit immensely from a relationship with their father regardless of whether or not I'm in agreement with his parenting style. I am not speaking about his legal or humanitarian rights here. I am speaking from pure, raw emotion and I'm capitalizing here on the fact that emotion need not be logical or rational.

I'm their mom. I'm the one who gave up my career and transformed every single aspect of my life to take on this all-encompassing role. I supported my husband by taking care of everything at home. I never ever called him and demanded that he come home from work. Well....just the one time when my newborn and my 2 year old seemed to be on a marathon of hysterical crying that went on perhaps not as long as it seemed at the time. I locked myself in the bathroom, cried and yes, I called my husband at 4pm and told him I needed help.

I told myself that I was a good wife, a good mother, and this was my job.

In those early, painful days, my thoughts would turn to very primitive thinking, and my thoughts in my head would sound something like, "it's not fair. Just because I'm no longer a wife, why do I have to be forced to play part-time Mommy ????" Again, these were thoughts in my head that I knew were irrational and which remained unspoken.

I was broken but my children were immune to this. This wasn't their problem to take on. Nearly 5 years later, I still have my moments. They're few and far between and my thought processes have evolved. I know in my heart that I'm not a part-time Mom. They're in my every thought. They know that, but I don't want to be in their every breath and every thought. This is not a healthy relationship for a child to form with a parent and as parents, we obviously want what's best for them. Our kids must feel secure and independent, and confident enough to have their own experiences independent of us.

I used to feel that it wasn't fair to be separated from my children every other weekend, but as parents, we MUST understand that this is the only fair arrangement. Children need time with both parents and if the parents aren't together, then this is the only way.

In the very early days, I used to feel that my ex had worked tirelessly earning his reputation in business and I earned my right to my kids. It's a tough thing to come to grips with, but the sooner we realize that this line of thinking is wrong, the sooner we're able to establish healthy boundaries for ourselves and for our children. Wanting to keep your children to yourself is not only misguided but it's actually dangerous to the overall wellbeing of your kids. My ex husband is a good dad. He's not perfect and he does things differently than me, but that doesn't make him or my children unentitled to a relationship. I am grateful that my children have 2 parents who love them and I am thrilled that they're able to share experiences with each of us.

If you're feeling possessive of your children, you need to seek expert help before you impart your unhealthy feelings onto your children. In the very early days, I was the one who needed to cope. I was the one who needed to find a better way and I did. I went for counselling to get a better perspective before my issues spilled over onto my children. I had centered my entire existence around my kids but there's a difference between healthy dedication to, and unhealthy dependence upon one's children. If you think that you may be crossing a line, take positive steps to correct it immediately. The best thing for your children is a healthy relationship with both parents. I can't stress this enough.

Balance. This is the ultimate goal. To achieve this, I had to force myself to step way back to that line. In the absence of a healthy marriage, I now see that I attached myself to my children wholly, fully, completely. They engulfed me. I lost who I was as a person, and defined myself solely as their mother. I now found myself with absolutely no identity on Tuesday nights and every other weekend.

Not healthy. Not cool. And certainly not an example I wanted to set for my kids. I and they deserved more.

I still miss them when they spend time with their dad but I know that it doesn't change my relationship with them. It doesn't take away from my role in their life, nor could it ever take away from their role in mine. It just redefines the role and that's a good thing. I know too, that their father offers them things that I don't. Allowing them to have their own relationship independent of me, is a wholistic approach to parenting which allows my children to grow in ways that they can't achieve from just one parent's involvement.

Stepping back and allowing my kids to form a relationship with their other parent from the beginning, when new boundaries are being established, is what's best for children. It's great for them and thankfully I have always allowed my rational and logical self to control my behavior in this regard.

It's sometimes tough to be without them, but I truly am happy when they call me and I hear in their voices that they're happy. I love listening to their stories about the adventures of their day. I love the laugh in their tone while they re-tell an animated version of their day's happenings. I know they're emotionally healthy and happy and they're developing in wonderful ways. I take pride in this, as does their father. They're our children and despite all else, their well-being takes precedence above all else. I know that they're growing up better rounded for all their experiences; even the ones they have without me, and I'm always glad that they want to share their stories with me.

When the issue of separation anxiety is yours alone, it's so important to acknowledge and identify it. If you're feeling this way, what's next? Finding a healthy outlet. Starting over. Getting to know you. Re-creating, tweaking, and re-defining who you are, as I had to do. Perhaps it's more a matter of finding an extension of who you are…one that is separate from being a parent. Create your own adventures and excitement and challenges that are independent of your children. You need to stand on your own and be you. And when you can do this, then you have truly grown from this divorce. Bad days are guaranteed. Re-construct the broken bits into a more whole version.

Dr. J. Says: Separation and divorce lead in most cases to two separate households, each of which your child will spend some time living in. What this means is there will be days or weeks of being separated from your child. This is another loss to grieve. Especially with young children you may not be used to not seeing your child for days at a time. You may be afraid of having no control or say in what goes on at their other home. Fear can creep in and make you cling to your children. They in turn can become afraid of leaving the more vulnerable parent alone. There is no right or wrong way to deal with separating from your child. Try to make it as fun an experience as possible and leave your fears to discuss with the co-parent in private. While missing your children is completely normal revolving your whole life around them is not. On days away from your kids use healthy coping techniques such as affiliation, exercise and activities to keep you from amplifying your fears. Having time apart will not damage your relationship with your children. And for them, learning they are ok without you is a powerful and important experience.

CHAPTER 7

Significant OTHERS (as in, other than you)

"I can't change the direction of the wind, but I can adjust my sails to always reach my destination."

— *Jimmy Dean*

Love changes everything. This we know. We're also painfully aware of the fact that divorce changes everything too. What happens then, when our ex finds love again? The answer is up to each of us.

When my kids came home shortly after their dad moved out, and told me "Daddy has a girlfriend" I was shocked. Not because it hadn't occurred to me that he would find someone rather quickly, but because my 7 year old baby was saying these words to me. This happened for me in stages. First, I had to get used to the fact that he had a girlfriend. Okay, I was cool with this. I was really handling things like a champ, as far as my kids and the outside world could tell. I chose to accept her, but at first I felt like she was in my life too. My closer circle and my heart knew that this wasn't exactly a seamless transition for me. I wasn't jealous of her per se, but it did make me feel a little insecure, that I could be so easily replaced. I knew logically, this was inevitable, but emotions are illogical.

The next stage is "We get to meet Daddy's girlfriend". This one for me was a bit tougher to swallow, but I was still handling it ok. I told my kids that she must be really special to Daddy if he wanted them to meet her. My kids felt that they could talk to me about her, and I took that as a positive…if they can talk to me about this, I must be doing a good job of making myself accessible and approachable. I listened and chimed in a few "that sounds so nice"'s when appropriate.

> Dr. J. Says: This may be a tough one to work through. Especially if questions of infidelity surround the new partner. Being hurt even if you were the one who asked for the divorce is normal. No one likes to feel they are so easily replaced. However targeting your anger at the new partner will only lead to your children doing the same. In these moments it is important to remember that your life is about YOU; not this other person. Their happiness does not change yours. So put the focus back where it belongs and work on yourself. With time these feelings will begin to lessen.

The meeting went rather smoothly and all seemed right in my world until the next stage was upon me…

"Daddy is taking us away for the weekend and his girlfriend is coming too". Ouch! The idea that SHE gets to spend a long weekend with my kids and I don't stung. What right does SHE have? Again, going back to my emotional self, my strongest argument was "it's not fair". Again, emotion failed to send the memo to logic.

The truth is that I have no control over what my ex-husband does with my kids or who he chooses to bring into their lives. He loves our children and he as I, only want what's best for them. We just don't always agree on what that is.

We need to accept this as part of the life experiences that they're now exposed to, and we have to believe that each person enriches their life in some way, small or large. It's ok. It's a good thing. We just have to hope that our former spouse has chosen someone with whom our children can get along because the alternative isn't good for anyone.

Dr. J. Says: Jealousy is a feeling we all like to pretend we don't have. But everyone experiences it at some time. The way to approach this is to ask yourself, "is there something I can change here?" Maybe you can organize a trip with your kids for another time so you don't feel left out. Maybe you can work on your health and fitness so you feel better about yourself. Once you feel back in control, the jealousy will likely turn into a distant memory.

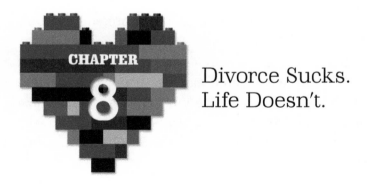

Divorce Sucks. Life Doesn't.

There is nothing good about divorce. I never expected to be here in my life. Who does? Growing up, I never heard about Prince Charming cheating on Cinderella because they lost their spark. I don't remember reading about how when Sleeping Beauty awoke from her slumber, she no longer recognized the woman she had become. I don't remember Prince Charming ever criticizing Cinderella for spending too much money on her glass slippers. Where in our stories did Snow White and her prince realize that their love was based on lies? When did Arielle begin to feel unappreciated? These are simply random examples used to make a point.

When we get married, we're all filled with love, excitement and hope for our future. Regardless of who or where we are, these are universal feelings. When we come to the cripplingly painful conclusion that our marriage is over, regardless of why, we find ourselves in uncharted, scary and choppy waters. This wasn't part of the plan. What happened? How did we get here? What's wrong with me? What's wrong with our former partner? What happened to us?

Dr. J. Says: Weddings are hopeful events filled with love, joy and promise. We tend to have unrealistic expectations of the true hard work of marriage based on fantasies or fairy tales. That you were hopeful on your wedding day is wonderful. It shows you have the capacity to be that way. Harness those feelings and use them as you push forward and shape your new future.

These are all normal questions that we ask ourselves, upon reflection. We may not be able to answer most of them, but we need to try. Divorce sucks. It really does. Regardless of circumstance, there's just nothing good about divorce. Hearts always break. Tears are always shed. Certain aspects are really ugly. The goal is to minimize the ugly so that we don't get sucked into a vortex of anger, resentment, bitterness or regret. We need to look at the past but not live in it. We need to look back in order to deconstruct our part in the breakdown of our marriage and why it didn't work. There are always two players in a divorce, irrespective of how you may feel like the victim. There is no minimizing one's pain, grief and anguish, but if we truly want to reconstruct our happy, we have to take a long, hard look at where we went wrong and actively decide what lessons we wish to carry into our new happily ever after. Plans always change, dreams sometimes shatter. This is divorce. It's ugly, it's complicated, it's raw and it's real.

Part Two

Kids and Co-Parenting

CHAPTER 9

Telling the Kids

"We're always bluffing, pretending we know best, when most of the time we're just praying we won't screw up too badly."

— Jodi Picoult, House Rules

Change is inevitable in life, but divorce is a change that my kids never asked for. They weren't given a choice. This life-altering, earth-shattering news was presented to them with absolutely no alternative or solution. My kids were so shocked when we broke the news to them. When we told them that we had to talk to them about something important, they honestly thought that they were going to have a new baby brother or sister! I mean seriously, they were completely clueless! Talk about breaking their little hearts. It was more than I could bear. We told them about it before dinner on a Friday, and then we made sure to spend the rest of the evening together. We were available to answer their questions and to show them that we were still a family. They were 7 and 9 at the time. The hours following were an emotional roller coaster for all of us.

They were excited at the prospect of having another house and bedroom to decorate at Daddy's. They were angry with both of us for making this choice. They were deeply sad that our family was changing forever. They were scared of the unknown (as was I!)

They asked a lot of questions, which I interpreted as a positive.

Communication is always key. (Funny, since it was the breakdown of communication that ultimately got me to this spot, but that's for another book).

That night, we decided to let the kids sleep in the same room as us. We had a pull-out cot that my ex-husband slept on, and the kids slept in bed with me. Throughout the night, they continued to ask questions. I remember one of my daughter's questions;

"Mommy, you know how sometimes we hear about a mom or dad who takes their kid away because they don't want the other parent to find them? Are you or daddy going to do that?"

I was so blown away by this question because it really showed me how scared my kids were. I was so thankful that we were there to answer the question right away, and that she didn't have to deal with this fear of parental abduction on her own in the middle of the night. We were able to put this concern to bed, once and for all.

This is pretty much the approach that I have taken with my kids in the weeks, months and years that followed that game-changing day. While the fear and uncertainty wore off as we all settled into our new normal, the questions changed and became fewer. There are still questions. There is still uncertainty, but these are indicative of life changes and growth, not necessarily of divorce. The lines do tend to get blurred in my opinion, and it becomes increasingly difficult to understand the source of your child's pain or anxiety. Is it normal growth and development or is it because of the divorce?

Dr. J. Says:

One of the most common reasons parents seek psychological help around the time of separation is in order to find the "right" way to tell the kids. Though there is no right way there are certain things you can do to make this experience easier on everyone.

1. Prepare what to say and tell them together. Kids need structure and certainty. Where will they live? How will things change? Make sure you know these details first and that you and your spouse are on the same page. Whatever your issues together this is the time to put them aside.

2. Let them ask their questions. Depending on the ages of your children their questions might run the range from " does this mean we are no longer a family" to "will my teddy bear live at daddy's house too" No question is stupid and ones that go unanswered can often lead to unnecessary fears in a child's mind.

3. Reassure them. Of your love. Of putting them first. Of it not being their fault. But don't be surprised if none of those things comes up as an issue in your child's conversation. Again depending on their developmental stage children can be very normally self-centered. They may be more concerned about their room and school than on the greater meaning. This is normal and the feelings may come later.

4. Watch the behavior. Your kids may seem fine after being told. But children often express feelings in their behavior. So make sure their teacher and caregivers are aware and to let you know of any changes. For children with pre-existing issues like Attention deficit or learning disabilities it may be useful to find out where they are at behaviorally prior to telling the child and it would be beneficial to involve their health care professionals so that any changes can be monitored.

CHAPTER
10

Kids

"As your kids grow up they may forget what you said, but they won't forget how you made them feel."

– Kevin Heath

My kids are my everything. They are amazing people who amaze me every day. I know that I have a very important job because they look to me for cues on how to behave and essentially, I play a pivotal role in shaping the types of people they become. I need to lead by example in every aspect of my life... No pressure...

The same is true and perhaps even more critical during a time of crisis. Divorce and separation is a crisis. It is a fundamental and devastating change in your family dynamic, that throws you and your entire family into crisis mode. How you choose to handle your crisis is entirely up to you. Do you panic and quickly start calling every health care professional you find on the internet? Do you suddenly find that wine plays a bigger role in your coping strategies? Do you lash out at friends and family because you're hurt and scared? Maybe you do none of these things, maybe you do some and maybe you have other behaviors that have surfaced since you realized that your marriage was falling apart. These changes incidentally, may not have just started with official separation. You may have been feeling and doing these things for many months or years prior. However, to your kids, it's new. You may feel relief at the idea that the marriage is ending. But I assure you, your kids don't. I saw it coming, but my kids didn't.

I felt a lot of deep sadness as I have talked about already, but I also felt a strange sense of relief. Relief that the stress of our marriage was over. Relief that I didn't have to have another discussion about how I make him feel and how he makes me feel. We really did give it a solid effort but in the end, the only thing we seemed to agree on, was that we weren't working anymore as a couple and we just couldn't get past whatever damage we had done to us and each other. We both needed to heal, but healing could only be done apart. We needed to transition and downgrade from life partners to parenting partners.

> Dr. J. Says: There are so many emotions one might feel when a marriage ends. Depending on the circumstances there may be relief in getting out of a difficult situation. There may be shock and disbelief if one partner was unaware of the other's discontent. Reminding yourself that there is no one way to feel is important. No matter how difficult it may be making sure you do not use your children as your source of support through these difficult feelings is crucial. Children cannot understand the nuances of adult relationships. If your child feels responsible for your well-being this puts a burden on them they are not ready for. If you are lonely, talk to friends. If you need someone to hug try a pet. Keep your relationship with your children as it has always been, with the adults in the driver's seat.

Our children were immune to all of this. Our marriage was one of complacency. We didn't fight. We didn't argue. We didn't yell or throw things at one another. To the outside world we had a solid marriage. I have heard that when parents break up, the children, while obviously sad are sometimes relieved that they no longer have to hear fighting. My children didn't have anything to be relieved about.

No matter how destructive a marriage is, children don't see it as unhealthy or destructive because that's all they've known. They don't know that things can be different. They don't know how to decipher healthy vs. unhealthy in terms of relationships. I can only talk about young children here, because that is my experience. My children couldn't understand or appreciate the nuances of their parents' relationship. They were immune to the tones in which we spoke to one another and the way we generally were around one another. I am not getting into details of my marriage here, not because I am hiding anything. It's simply not the purpose of this book. My opinions of my relationship are subjective and admittedly skewed by time passed, emotion and my own subjectivity. To re-hash the details of my marriage from my recollection would be counter-productive. I have moved forward. I want to encourage you to move forward. Once we made the decision to end our marriage, there was no looking back, except to reflect and learn from it. Life is always propelling us forward. If we don't move forward, then we miss out on living life.

Dr. J. Says: Our first role models of what it is to be a man or woman come from our parents. It's no surprise that our first model of a real relationship comes from them too. Even though clearly your marriage did not work out, children can still learn to have healthy relationships by how you act in the aftermath. Are you respectful? Do you put down your ex? How you handle conflict? Though you may not like your ex, showing them respect and caring goes a long way in teaching your children how to have loving and fulfilling relationships.

CHAPTER
11

Divorce Pains vs. Growing Pains; Understanding My Kids

"When you take the time to actually listen with humility, to what people have to say, it's amazing what you can learn. Especially if the people who are doing the talking also happen to be children."

– Greg Mortenson

I tended to attribute every behavior and every mood to the divorce. When my daughter began to experience troubles with some of her girlfriends, I immediately feared it was because of the divorce. OMG...she can no longer form healthy friendships, she doesn't want to be friends with so-and-so...OMG I've taught her that it's ok to give up on relationships! I've ruined my child! NOT SO!

It had more to do with the fact that my daughter was now 10 and a half, and girl drama sets in regardless of parents' marital status. Girls will be girls. I needed to keep things in perspective and stop looking at everything through my divorce glasses. Rose-colored glasses are deceptive, as are muddy ones. Divorce glasses are muddy glasses. Clean them off and look at each situation with clarity. Some situations do present themselves because of divorce, but I found that it's not the divorce per se that hurts your children. It's how they see their parents handling it. Do they see Mommy and Daddy as a united front? Do they see fighting, disrespect and belittlement? Do they have to listen to negative talk about one parent from the other? These are mental health breakers!!! Don't do it! It's tempting to tell your kids that you're on edge because Mommy is threatening to not give you any money or that Daddy is threatening to take the kids away from you or whatever other garbage happens during your divorce process. Don't do it! This is the stuff that creates problems for your kids. Divorce doesn't screw up kids. Parents do. Just because you've made the decision to divorce (or even if the decision was made for you), you haven't messed up your kids. Their fate is not sealed. The way you conduct yourself and handle things from this point forward is what will determine your child's well-being, much more so than the divorce itself.

Dr. J. Says: It is difficult for a parent to know when a change in their child is due to the stress of the divorce or a normal change in development. Since we know from research in the area most children do in fact adapt well after divorce it is important to deal with the change as just that, a change. Talking to your child, getting the school involved and getting help if needed are all steps you would take as a parent. And just because you are separating, this is no different. If your child is refusing to go to school, not playing with friends or not sleeping and eating as before you may want to seek help sooner rather than later to see if your child is having a difficult time with things. You know your children best and should not be afraid to seek help. It's a tough time for everyone.

The best thing to do to help your child go through their own grieving process is to let them express their feelings. Don't feel the need to rush them through any stage. If they are angry give them safe ways to express it (writing a letter, punching a pillow, counting to 10, deep breathing). It is hard for parents to watch their children dealing with difficult emotions but remember the younger they learn how to cope with these feelings successfully, the better they will face challenges in adulthood.

Divorce is an unfortunate part of life. It's how we choose to cope and manage that will set our path. Our children look to us to set examples and to obtain cues on how to feel and how to act. I was going through my own private hell. But I put on a happy, positive front for my kids. Did they ever see me cry? Of course they did, and this isn't a bad thing. I would say that I was having a sad moment.

> Dr. J. Says: Though expressing feelings in front of your child is fine, depending on them as a source of support is not. Children will look to you to guide their response. If you feel the divorce is "the end of the world". your child may as well. Keeping a positive and open attitude is important. Keeping regular routines is too. If these tasks are too difficult for you, then seeking psychological help so that you can continue to be a parent is a great idea.

Exercise: How Do You Talk To Your Kids About Sadness?

Here's how I explained sadness to my 7 year old boy and my 9 year old girl:

Think of our feelings as a NASCAR...most of the time, we're good. We go to school, we have playdates, we spend time with family, we do homework, and we're happy. We're good. Think of our sadness as a pit-stop. Every once in a while we need to take a break. We need to stop, take a break and be sad. That's ok. Sadness is healthy, and it's normal. But if we stay in our pit-stop for too long, we fall behind and we miss a lot of the good stuff ahead. Take pit-stops when you need them, but then jump back in the race, and when you do that, you'll race stronger and harder because your pit-stop gave you strength. I use this analogy for myself too. It may sound silly, but for me and my kids, it works. 2 years later, we're all still using this and we talk about our feelings.

Dr. J. Says: Sadness is an important part of grieving a loss. Your child may describe it as a "tummy ache", "funny feeling" or just show it through tears. Knowing when your child is sad and letting them express it to you is the key. After they have expressed how they are feeling it is good to point out that all feelings are temporary and come and go. Providing positive things to look forward to or that happened that day can help a child learn to balance the negative with the positive. If your child is unable to stop experiencing sadness however it may be time to get outside help.

What are some relevant analogies that you can use with your kids:

_____

_____

_____

_____

_____

CHAPTER 12

The "Co" in Co-Parenting means Cooperative… Not Competitive!

"Divorce isn't the child's fault. Don't say anything unkind about your ex to the child, because you're really just hurting the child."

— *Valerie Bertinelli*

I love my time with my kids! For me, my time with them is to be cherished. It's my time to soak up every moment with them. Enjoy their stories, their gestures, their playing. Right? Absolutely, but then there's real life…homework, sibling fights, bedtime negotiations, discipline, after-school activities, dinner, play dates, work, bills, deadlines and the list goes on. But this is MY time with the kids. I want to just do great things with them.

The reality is, I can't look at my time with the kids as "my time". It's *their* time. In keeping my objectives clear and always put the kids first, I must realize that it's not about me. It's as always, about them! Do I love that my daughter will sleep over at a friend's house when I only get to see her every other weekend? Of course not, but if her dad and I were still married, would I prevent her from going? Absolutely not, so what right do I have to stop her or make her feel guilty now? Absolutely none. This is her time to be a kid. If my kids want to sleep at a friend's house, or have a playdate with a friend, then how am I acting in their best interest, if I deny them this rite of passage? It would be unfair and selfish, and it would discount the vital role that socialization and friendships play in our children's lives.

While tempting, it's important not to fall into the trap of being the "fun parent". There should never be a sense of competition between parents. You're not trying to out-do the other one. You're both parenting your children. This involves homework and discipline and responsibilities. Don't put those aside in an effort to want to get your kids to enjoy their time with you more. You and your ex's finances may look very different. What you buy for your children (aside from necessities) is unimportant. What you give your children in terms of values, love, guidance and security is far more valuable than anything you can purchase.

> Dr. J. Says: Bribing your children or over indulging them to win affection only leads to problems with your kids later on. Kids thrive with boundaries and routines. If they learn they can have whatever they want how will they grow to be adults who can tolerate disappointments? As much as possible, keep the routines and rules the same across both households. Remember you are doing this for your kids. This is not about punishing or being more loved, than your ex.

I have heard Beverly Cathcart-Ross speak several times.

Beverley is a speaker with schools and corporations. Her advice can be found in magazines such as Today's Parent, Readers Digest, Canadian Family, and Chatelaine. Beverley was hailed "Toronto's top parenting guru" by Toronto Life magazine. She co-wrote "Raising Great Parents - How to Become the Parent Your Child Needs You to Be"; and she produced a series of Parenting CD's such as Self Esteem, What's your Style, Who's the Boss, Keeping the Peace and Setting Limits. More information about Beverly can be found on her website at ParentingNetwork.ca. I generally find her parenting tips quite helpful but her concept of parenting for the long-term as opposed to the short-term has really resonated and has essentially changed my outlook on, and method of parenting.

You may not love your kids' dad or mom, but they do, and they should! Fast forward 20 years. When my kids sit around talking about their childhood to their friends, I want my kids to be the ones to know they were loved by both parents, and both parents provided them with a good, solid foundation, however different these look. How would it be beneficial to my kids long term, to be sitting there 20 years from now saying "my mom was great but my dad didn't really spend much time with us?" That does not create a healthy, well-balanced adult. I try to parent keeping this long-term objective in mind. I find that focusing on the long term goal helps to eliminate some of the daily frustrations and noise that arise.

For example, when my son asks to go to a football game with his dad on a Sunday that happens to fall on my weekend, I don't love it but I understand that his favourite team doesn't come to town regularly and I don't want to stand in the way of allowing him to experience this with his dad. Am I missing out on a Sunday afternoon with my son? Yes, but long term, does this really matter? I'm not suggesting that we disregard our parenting schedule, nor do I feel that these changes should become a regular practise, but children can benefit from flexibility. This flexibility needs to obviously be reciprocated but in the long run, our children will be well adjusted.

Dr. J. Says: Research strongly supports the idea that children thrive when they have a positive relationship with both parents. While you can't control the other parent's behavior, you can control how you speak about them and behave towards them. Putting your ex down is telling your children they are one half bad. Remember that. Giving your child reasons to feel badly about themselves was not the goal of your divorce. Make the experience as easy for them as possible and keep the negative talk away from your kids. They hear everything.

When my kids are with me, I obviously want to only create happy memories, but life often has other plans. I rarely yell; it's just not my style and I happen to be fairly patient...most of the time. My children and I obviously go through the regular struggles and battles that normal kids and parents go through, regardless of my marital status. I want my children to see me get angry when the situation calls for it. I want them to be angry with me too. Why? Because this is normal and if they're never exposed to this, then how can they ever learn to work through it? Negative emotions are part of growth because we need to equip our kids with the tools to resolve and to come through adversity strong. Remember it's ultimately about them, not you. Look at the big picture. Our long-term goal as parents is to raise happy, healthy, well-adjusted people.

> Dr. J. Says: Children need to learn how to deal with positive and negative emotions. Fear, sadness and disappointment are a normal part of adult life. Every time your child goes through a difficult time they are developing skills for later on in life. Just as you train your muscles to get stronger, coping with adversity trains your brain.

Real life parenting is tough. It's important to work through tough stuff with them so that they learn how to work through it for themselves. This is long-term parenting. I don't see myself as a single parent. I still have a co-parenting partner. Our relationship needed to be re-defined. I'm not doing this alone (though sometimes I wish I were, as I'm sure he does). I still have to consult with him when it comes to major decisions pertaining to our children. I am single, in that I'm not married. But I'm not a single parent. I had so much autonomy when we were married, and I often resent the fact that I now have to consult with him on major decisions, but I understand logically that this is the way it must be. This is part of the control that I had to learn to give up when we divorced.

> Dr. J. Says: The better you and your ex can put your differences aside, the easier it will be for your kids to adapt. Conflict creates negative feelings in parents and children. When there are important decisions to be made, try to put your ego aside and truly focus on what is best for the children. Try to still present a unified front so that children don't learn to split you and manipulate the situation to their advantage. Being the most beloved parent is not worth the cost to your kids.

"I hate you. I'm going to live with Daddy"

I've heard many people tell me that they don't discipline their children nearly as much once they're separated. In my opinion, it's because they're afraid that their kids will call their other parent and complain, or they want to be seen as the superior parent. Human nature may persuade us to bask in the glory that for that one brief moment, we're the favorite parent when our children prefer us. I get it. I really do, but so what? So my kids will call their dad and say "Mommy is being so mean!" Do I love it when my kids do this? Of course not. I cringe when they threaten to call him but I hand them the phone. It's certainly not a good Mommy moment for me, but in a way, it is because I am not afraid to parent my children. I think that when we become afraid to parent our children, we are failing them.

> Dr. J. Says: Discipline, boundaries and routine make kids feel safe and secure. Don't think that by relaxing the rules, this is helping your child feel better. It is actually having the opposite effect. If you feel you are having trouble effectively parenting your children seek help from a professional.

When my kids call me crying, saying "Mommy, I hate Daddy. He's so rude!" am I tempted to say, "I know, but Mommy is here for you". What would it teach my kids if I gave into this temptation? Remember that one day soon, the tables will be turned and you'll be the unfavorable parent of the moment. Don't fall prey to this trap…it's a dangerous one. Bearing in mind that our ultimate goal as a parent is to provide our children with life skills, this is a perfect opportunity for you to teach them about conflict resolution. Regardless of what I want to say, I listen to them as they vent to me, and then I tell them that they need to work this out with Daddy. "It sounds like you and Daddy need to talk about this once you've calmed down. Is there anything you need from me to help you calm down?"

This way, they know that I can be their judgment-free sounding board. I'm also not giving them an easy 'out'. They know that they need to work it out. Conflict resolution is a life skill and now's my chance to teach it to my children. It's not about me, it's about them, and giving them the tools to manage and work through conflict is a wonderful gift to give them.

I know from experience, that this is much easier said than done, but believe me, it will be worth it! Because you're co-parenting, you and your ex need to present a united front. I don't always agree with his parenting style or his methods, but the same is true of married couples. I have to respect that when the kids are with him, he needs to deal with these issues and when they're with me, the responsibility falls upon me. Presenting a united front however, shows the kids that they can't just run to the other parent when they don't like something. They need to stick it out and deal with it. This skill will serve them well in life.

If your ex doesn't quite take this approach, so be it. Remember that you're not doing it for your ex; you're doing it for your kids. If we could all just take our anger and hurt out of the equation when dealing with our kids, we would find that things tend to run much smoother. You have nothing to lose by trying this method, but you and your kids have everything to gain.

One of the most valuable lessons that I'm learning is to take the emotion out of divorce. It sounds utterly ridiculous. I can think of no other situation or predicament that is by its very nature, more emotionally charged than a divorce, but when it comes to decision making within a divorced situation (or any life situation for that matter) stripping the emotion from your choice will help you make the right choice. I tell my kids all the time, "Doing the right thing is not always the easy thing" and in most cases, doing what's right is even harder.

We all know that we shouldn't involve our children in our arguments because it can create irreparable psychological damage to our children, yet most of us are guilty of it, in one form or another; married or divorced. So why do we engage or why are we tempted to engage in this? Why are we knowingly placing our children in a situation that we know hurts them? It's all in the rationalization. It's all about how we rationalize and justify our choices. I can't tell you how many times I've heard, "Ya, but they need to understand why I'm so upset". NO! They don't require any type of explanation that involves negative talk about their parent. Regardless of how you justify it for your own conscience, it's wrong. Stop doing it. Nothing good can come from parental alienation. Nothing. This is why you need to take the emotion out of it. Step back from your own situation. No judgment here, I assure you, but we need to look at our situation with a bird's eye view so that we can get some perspective. I'm 40 years old and to this day, when my mom says something negative to me about my dad, I cringe. My parents have been married to each other for 45 years and the fact that they're married, and the fact that I'm an adult, doesn't make it any easier to hear. Imagine now, that I was a child and I didn't have the coping tools that I do. How would it feel then? Unimaginable. This is what we do to our kids when we tell ourselves that we're just "enlightening" them or "explaining" it to them. Don't! They don't require such explanations nor do they require enlightenment. It hurts them! Plain and simple. If you take nothing else from this book, please take this. If you're reading this thinking, "ya, but..." then please stop. There are no buts about this! NONE.

Dr. J. Says: Parental alienation syndrome has been talked about more and more in recent days. It is the process by which one parent deliberately turns the children against the other parent often leading to loss of contact with that other parent. Besides the legal implications, the psychological effects of brainwashing your child can be severe. If you feel you are headed down this path stop and get help. There is no greater harm you can do to your child right now than depriving them of a loving parent. If you have something negative to say about your ex, write it down. Feel free to talk to other supportive adults. Involve your lawyer if you truly believe your ex is displaying behavior that puts you children at risk. But remember that by putting down your ex, you are putting down your child. And one day they may be unable to forgive you for it.

Just for Fun:

New Years' Disillusions Vs. Year Round Resolutions

New Years' comes along once a year and some of us have all these grand ideas that we're going to do things differently. We're going to set goals to become better versions of ourselves. While the intent of a resolution is a great idea, most of us revert back to our old ways sometime in January or February.

Getting divorced is a wonderful opportunity to create some resolutions for yourself, regardless of season or date. My general rule for a resolution is to make it small, simple easy to follow through with. Make it something that will create positivity in your everyday life. Here are some ideas:

1. Keep a journal and write down one thing each day that you're grateful for.

2. Try one new recipe a month. You may find a few new favorites.
3. Reach out to an old friend from whom you've drifted apart.
4. Perform one random act of kindness each week.
5. Pack a little note in your child's lunch box every once in a while.
6. Remember to say "thank you" to those in the service industry, even if it's for something small like wiping your table or refilling your water glass.
7. Try one new thing each month.

Add your own:

You can't change who you are, nor should you want to. You can however, certainly improve your outlook and make improvements to who you are along your journey to becoming who you want to be.

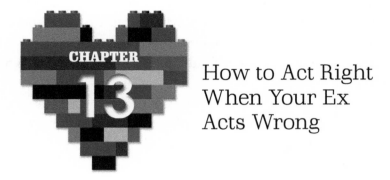

CHAPTER

13

How to Act Right
When Your Ex
Acts Wrong

"Sometimes life hits you in the head with a brick. Don't lose faith."

– *Steve Jobs*

We tell ourselves that we don't want to involve the kids and we've heard every parenting expert discuss the damaging effects of child involvement in grown up issues and parental alienation, but if our ex is doing it, do we need to set the record straight? We don't have to lower ourselves to that. For example, when you're buying your child new shoes for school, and while all you expect is a simple "thank you", you get ...Thank you for what? Mom/Dad gives you money to pay for all our stuff"

What do you say? How do you resist the urge to "set them straight" or defend yourself?

We all know WHAT to do in this situation. We rise above it and we continue being the pillar of all that is strong and right for our children. The WHAT is the easy part. The HOW however, can be a bit tricky. It's so easy for people on the outside to tell us what to do and how to behave, and judge us when we suffer the inevitable minor (and sometimes not so minor) slips. It's easy to know how but it takes a real strength and commitment to actually do it and know how to do it.

HEATHER TANNENBAUM

I truly believe that talking openly and honestly with kids is fundamental. However, there's a balance that ought to be found between the truth and inappropriate information.

A reply to your kids when they said that "Mom/Dad gives you money to take care of us", can simply be this:

"Yes, it's true that Mommy/Daddy gives me money each month. That's the law. She/He has to give me money each month because when we were married, we agreed that it would be best for our family if I stayed home with you and she/he worked without my help in bringing money into our family".

Would I ever feel the need or be comfortable discussing legalities of my divorce with my kids? Absolutely not but sometimes the need for a dose of unbiased, fact-based information free from opinion is ok. There are many opportunities when these types of dilemmas present themselves. As divorced parents, we need to step outside of our emotions and react in a healthy way for our kids.

It's heartbreaking to hear parents' words through the mouths of their children. We've all probably experienced this. I've heard a young girl describe her father as "just a sperm donor". This girl was not even old enough to know what she was saying…To be clear, this was not my child.

I heard another girl tell me that her dad is a "dead beat"…again, I'm certain that she's repeating what she's heard her mother say. These are unfair, unhealthy and inappropriate burdens to saddle our kids with.

Exercise:

Saying What You Want vs. Saying What You Should

Examples that are not necessarily based on personal experiences.

Example A:

"Daddy says he won't take me shopping on our vacation because you didn't give me spending money".

What You May Want to Say:

You're on vacation with Daddy. This is his time with you. This is HIS obligation.

What You Should Say:

I'm sorry that Daddy won't take you shopping. That would have been really nice but I'm sure there are other fun things that Daddy has planned while you're away.

Example B:

"Daddy says that we don't eat home cooked meals at your house:

What You May Want to Say:

Well, it's none of Daddy's business what you eat here. If he wanted you to eating home cooking, then he shouldn't have walked out on me.

What You Should Say:

Well, that's part of the fun of having 2 homes. Daddy has things that he's good at which includes cooking. Here we get to do other things that are different than when you're with Daddy.

Example C:

"I hate Mommy's new boyfriend. He's so rude and he's always around"

What You May Want to Say:

Ya, I didn't get a good feeling about him either. Why your mother would be with that loser is beyond me.

What You Should Say:

Have you spoken to Mommy about how you feel? He's obviously very important to Mommy so maybe give him a chance. If you still don't like him, you should talk to Mommy about it. She would want to know how you feel.

You often have to think quickly and in the moment in order to allow yourself to go straight for the right response. If you're not quick on your feet or if your child has totally caught you off guard, there's nothing wrong with telling them that you want to discuss this with them, but a bit later. This way you're not dismissing their openness but you're giving yourself some time to process and come up with an appropriate response.

Write Down Some of Your Own:

Part Three

Friendship

CHAPTER 14

Friends

There are defining moments in one's life when we call on our supportive troops to step forward and be there for us; our friends. I found the months following my separation to be very eye-opening in terms of who my friends really were and who they weren't. Some friends really stepped up and went above and beyond for me. They continue to lend me a listening ear, a supportive shoulder or words (sometimes harsh) that I need to hear.

There are those people too, who were great friends as long as life was easy. They either were too uncomfortable or simply didn't know how to be the type of friend I needed, and that's alright. There are all sorts of people in one's life. Different people offer and bring different things into your life.

I have many friends in my world, but only a select special few in my life. These select few keep my secrets, feel my pain, they celebrate my joys and they're always there when I need them. Before my separation however, I didn't feel that I had any friends like the ones I have just described. I was so blocked off emotionally from everyone that I had failed to see the value that these special people bring to my life. I had to take an emotional leap of faith. I had to trust, and I had to ask for help. I had to acknowledge and reveal vulnerability. Not weakness, but vulnerability. It wasn't all rainbows and unicorns. There were a few people who disappointed me but I realized that this had nothing to do with me. They simply didn't have the capacity to be what or who I needed. I could move forward with the satisfaction that I had put myself out there.

It was a process, but the beautiful friendships that I have cultivated by believing in these people have really been invaluable to me. They, along with my family, have been my unwavering support. You need this support!! If you don't already have it, get it! Friends and family are key in the divorce process. Take a leap of faith, go out on a limb and ask for help from a select few. There are certain people in your world that need to be in your life.

Dr. J Says:

Affiliation is a coping technique in which the individual deals with emotional conflict or internal or external stressors by turning to others for help or support. This involves sharing problems with others but does not imply trying to make someone else responsible for them. This has been shown to be one of the best ways to cope with stressful times.

Whether friends, family or a support group, leaning on others during this time is not only ok it's psychologically healthy.

If you're not sure how to find a support group in your area, start with a simple internet search. You can also ask your divorce lawyer if they have any support groups that they can refer you to. There are also many websites that offer divorce resources, and these can lead you to therapists or support groups. If you know of anyone who has gone through a divorce and you're comfortable asking, they may know of a group.

Some friendship quotes to make you smile:

1. "It is one of the blessings of old friends that you can afford to be stupid with them" Ralph Waldo Emerson

2. "A real friend is one who walks in when the rest of the world walks out" Walter Winchell
3. "Friendship...is not something you learn in school. But if you haven't learned the meaning of friendship, you really haven't learned anything" Muhammad Ali
4. "A single rose can be my garden...a single friend, my world." Leo Buscaglia

Quotes 1–4 from BrainyQuote

5. There is nothing better than a friend, unless it is a friend with chocolate." Linda Grayson
6. "Friends are people who know you really well and like you anyway." Greg Tamblyn
7. "Friends give you a shoulder to cry on. But best friends are ready with a shovel to hurt the person who made you cry." Unknown
8. "Sometimes me think, 'What is friend?' Then me say, 'Friend is someone to share the last cookie with'." Cookie Monster
9. "Lots of people want to ride with you in the limo, but what you want is someone who will take the bus with you when the limo breaks down." Oprah Winfrey

Quotes 5-9 from curatedquotes.com

Being a Good Friend

"And as the years go by
Our friendship will never die
You're gonna see it's our destiny
You've got a friend in me"

Randy Newman - You've Got A Friend
In Me Lyrics | MetroLyrics

In order to have good friends as described last chapter, you need to ***be*** a good friend. Obvious, right? Isn't this what we tell our kids when we see or hear them reacting to a friend in a not-so pretty moment? Of course it goes for us too. How can we, during this turbulent time in our life, possibly be a good friend to others? We can, and we should for a few reasons.

Being a good friend can be self-fulfilling.

We sometimes need distraction. Certainly I did, and still do on occasion. Being there for a friend, listening to what's going on with them and helping them, is somewhat therapeutic. It re-directs your focus away from you (which may be very welcome sometimes) and it allows you to help someone else, subsequently making you feel better about your value. You're able to help others. This was huge for me, because most times, I felt quite inconsequential and insignificant. Helping others made me feel good about myself. I felt that I had some purpose, in a life that was in upheaval. This made me feel valued.

Refelection Exercice:

What kind of friend are you? Check all that apply and circle all that you wish to work on:

Kind	Trustworthy	Loyal	Thoughtful
Compassionate	Understanding	Reliable	Easy Going
Good listener	Non Judgemental	Honest	Flexible
Good Hugger	Funny/Sense of Humor	Fun	Transparent
Loving	Respectful	Lets You Be You	Forgiving
Common Interests	Down to Earth	Approachable	Unconditional love
Insightful			

Add you own:

Mutual Friends

> "Friendship - that mutual affection and companionship between people - is arguably one of the most important aspects of life."
>
> *Ann Williams, 101 Friendship Quotes*

Another, perhaps less obvious way to be a good friend, is to not make our friends choose sides! During the course of your relationship with your ex, you more than likely accumulated some mutual friends. Perhaps as couples or simply as individuals. Now that you're no longer together, your friends may feel uneasy, uncomfortable, and may likely proceed with caution where you're concerned.

When my ex and I split up, we were amicable, and we made sure that our friends knew this. We told our friends that we didn't expect them to take sides or even have to listen to any banter about one another. It simply wouldn't be fair of us. We shared mutual friends; couples, individuals and family friends. We didn't want to make it awkward for anyone.

Despite our efforts to communicate our objectives to our friends, people still backed off. Nobody was quite sure what to make of our promises and they seemed uneasy and guarded. Our friends instinctually and understandably, tended to tread lightly and very cautiously for the first while. This was painful to me. My entire world was uncertain and this extended further than I had anticipated. I felt that I was on shaky ground and having people feel uncomfortable around me was hurtful.

I completely understood and appreciated my friends' feelings and I absolutely understood their initial hesitation. I figured that in time, our friends would see that we were capable of keeping our private issues to ourselves. I certainly lost some friends along the way that he remains close to but it's all par for the course I think. I am pleased that most of our mutual friends are still mutual friends, and it's been really helpful in making the transition more seamless for the kids. My relationship with my ex isn't as amicable as it once was, but I'm pleased that I'm able to keep it out of our mutual friendships.

Whether you're amicable or not with your ex, it's important for you to tell your mutual friends that you don't want to put them in an awkward spot. Whether your ex chooses to have this conversation with them too, is irrelevant. You need to not assume that your friends know this. You'll want to reassure them that you don't expect nor want them to choose sides. There are no sides really. If you're able to do this, your mutual friends will appreciate it, and you will be able to maintain positive relationships with people in your life.

Neither my ex nor I stopped making plans with our mutual friends, nor should we have. There were times that my friends would be going over with their family, to my ex's house on the weekend for a BBQ with my kids and his new girlfriend. It seemed a bit strange to me at first, and I admittedly felt left out, but ultimately, that's the nature of divorce. Above all, I was thrilled for my kids that they were enjoying a day with friends regardless of whether I was there or not. I made sure to tell my friends this, so that there was no awkwardness. I would send a text thanking them for giving my kids a great afternoon or evening, and I sincerely meant it!

We often get together with mutual friends and we always have a great time, because I never make it about the divorce. There are so many better things to talk about, and so many happier ways to spend time with friends.

Do not make your friends choose. It's awkward, it's unfair and in the end, it's a sure-fire way to alienate your friends. I'm not referring to your core group, but specifically to your mutual friends. This is tough, but don't expect your friend to keep things from her husband or his wife. If you're confiding in your girlfriend or guy friend, don't ask or expect that they will withhold this information from their partner. It's simply unfair. Perhaps they will, perhaps they won't, but it's entirely their prerogative. If you're going to confide in a friend, expect that they may tell her husband or he will tell his wife. Operate with this expectation. Anything else would be an unfair burden for you to place upon your friend.

Part Four

Moving Forward
and Rebuilding

CHAPTER 17

Reprogramming Yourself

"If nothing ever changed, there'd be no butterflies."

– unknown

Divorce brings out the ugly in all of us, and your divorce process is going to be very different than anyone else's, yet not so different at all. Here's what we all share:

Divorce Incongruities:

There are times when we feel strong and in control,

And times when we mourn our marriage and our pre-separation life.

There are times we're proud of how far we've come,

And times we're ashamed of how far we haven't.

We have times of great epiphanies and self-revelations,

And times of great sadness and self-doubt.

Sometimes we feel we can handle it,

Sometimes we feel we can't.

Sometimes we feel the kids are doing great and we take pride in their well being,

And times we feel like complete failures.

We all have times of peace within ourselves and with our ex,

And times of stress and conflict within ourselves and others.

Advantage: we still know how to push our ex's buttons

Disadvantage: he/she still knows how to push ours.

The trick is to reprogram yourself. Reprogramming ourselves is what I think is the key to our inner peace and our happiness. It takes away any emotional power people have over us, and it puts the power back in our hands. We choose our buttons and we don't allow anyone to push them.

Reprogram yourself, and you'll essentially reprogram your life. It's an internal process and it takes a shit-load of work; hard work, but....once you've learned how to do this, then you are your own person. You have taken control of you. This is a powerful force, don't give it away and don't let others deflate your inner power. It's there, and it's up to you to find it.

I'll give you a personal example. I'm a very reactionary person. When someone does something that I don't like, I tend to get angry. I could never differentiate my feelings. Whether I was hurt, sad, angry, betrayed, it all manifested as anger and as my defence mechanism, I would lash out. This was my greatest challenge in my reprogramming process.

I had to step back and learn to identify what it was that I was feeling. It sounds very juvenile and very much like an exercise you would do with a 3 year old, but nonetheless, there I was, trying to sort through all of these emotions. How did I do it? I sat back and did nothing when I was confronted with a negative situation or put in a negative position. I said nothing. I did what appeared to be nothing, when in fact I was actually doing a lot of work. I left the situation (physically got up and left, or hung up the phone, stepped away from my email, put my phone away) whatever I needed to do to actually remove myself from the situation.

I went to a quiet, safe spot (usually my car or home) and I sat. Sometimes for hours. To the onlooker, it would have seemed that I was doing nothing more than sitting in a trance like state, and I suppose I was, but inside, I was hard at work, doing some pretty heavy lifting. I sorted through what had happened, I replayed it in my mind. And then I asked myself, "How do I feel"? I would literally go through a mental list of emotions, checking off which ones applied to this situation. Was I angry? Hurt? Betrayed? Embarrassed? Ashamed? Insulted?

Once I had identified which feelings I was experiencing, I needed to justify to myself why I was feeling those feelings. As trivial as it may seem, this was one of the fundamental keys to my healing and taking control of the only thing I could; myself. I needed to give myself permission to feel these things. I had shut off all my emotions for so long, that this was an important part of my re-programming. I had to tap into these emotions and not only understand them, but I had to learn what to do with them.

Once I had identified what was going on inside of me, and given myself permission to feel, I was able to figure out how to respond in a way that appropriately conveyed my feelings. This takes time. And it's for this reason that I never respond to a stressful situation for at least 24 hours. In 24 hours, your entire perspective changes. As Don Henley sang, "In a New York minute....everything can change. In a New York minute..."

An interesting thing began to happen...I was no longer out of control. I was no longer exacerbating a bad situation by reacting emotionally to it. I took my time and I figured out not only how I felt and why, but also how to react in a calm way. I was in complete control of my feelings and my actions. I took the power away from those who had been pushing my buttons. I was now at the control switch. The buttons had been replaced.

I was choosing how to react and when. This is a very empowering phenomenon. The only person who now pushes my buttons, is me. It's tough sometimes, and I still physically and emotionally step back from a potentially volatile situation, but I do. It's important for me because that's how I am able to re-group and figure out how to deal with the situation presented to me. We always have choices. I don't always make the right ones, but by giving myself some time and space to re-group, I am making much better and well thought out decisions, than when I would simply be emotionally reactionary. Emotions are important to identify and nurture, and while they have an important place in our hearts, emotions should know their place. It's in our hearts and not our minds. Once our minds begin to be controlled by our emotions, we have lost all sense of logic and reason. Learning to stay in control of your emotions and your actions is key to taking back control of yourself and moving forward. This is a major step in reconstructing your happy.

CHAPTER 18

A Theme Song

Who can turn the world on with her smile?
Who can take a nothing day, and suddenly make it all seem worthwhile?
Well it's you girl, and you should know it
With each glance and every little movement you show it ...

http://www.stlyrics.com/lyrics/
televisiontvthemelyrics-50s60s70s/
marytylermooreshow.htm

This idea was first introduced to me on the hit TV show Ally McBeal, when Ally's psychiatrist told her that she needed a theme song. It's so true! I'm not sure if this is a typical psychiatric approach, but I gave it a try, and it works.

Have a theme song. Pick a song or make a playlist that makes you feel empowered. Built of songs that speak to you and boost you up. Ever notice that when you're falling in love, every song on the radio is directed at you? When you're going through a divorce or a break up, all the songs seem to be telling your story? When I was trying to re-program myself, all the songs I heard were about empowerment and strength, and hearing these songs helped me to not feel so alone. I know that Katy Perry didn't write "Firework" or "Roar" for me, but at the time, it kind of felt like she did. Even the theme song to The Mary Tyler Moore Show" spoke to me, and I heard it differently than ever before. Hearing and listening to songs of empowerment made me feel stronger and empowered, so I started listening to them more. I would blast them in the car, and on my computer, or during my workouts. I would dance to them with my kids and sing them out loud. These songs still give me the lift that I sometimes need to get through whatever it is that I need to get through. These songs help us change the narrative in our heads and we should never underestimate the power of our thoughts.

Exercise: Some theme songs that work for you:

_____

_____

_____

_____

CHAPTER

19

Rebuilding Myself

"Someday, someone will hug you so tight, that all your broken pieces fit back together"

– Unknown

Part of my rebuilding process extends to changing characteristics about me that need changing. For example, I have always been a pleaser...I have a very difficult time saying "no" to people, even when I know that what they're asking of me is unfair or unreasonable. I also have a tendency to go above and beyond, when it comes to helping someone. I don't necessarily believe that the ladder is a weakness of mine. I've simply learned not to expect reciprocity from others. I do it because it makes me feel good to do, and as long as I'm aware of the fact that most people aren't likely to go to such lengths for me, that's ok. I've come to learn that this isn't a reflection on me, but rather, on them. I've learned that it's important to understand each of my friends' capacities and know exactly what they're willing to do and what they're willing not to do for me. Each relationship is different, and understanding what you give to and get from the other person is a key element to figure out. For example, I know exactly who I can count on to pick my kids up from school if I'm in a pinch, and I know who I wouldn't call for such a task. Not because they're bad friends, but because it's just not something they would do.

I wasn't able to really identify and reconstruct this, until I really examined myself after my separation. I took stock of who I am, who I'm not, who I want to be, and who I don't. That's what this process is all about. I had to re-invent myself in order to prevent myself from continuing and repeating the same patterns.

Meeting New People, Friends and Others

"The process of divorce is about loading that blanket, throwing it up, watching it all spin, and worrying what stuff will break when it lands."

— Amy Poehler

From the moment word of my separation hit the grapevine, it seemed that everyone had someone they wanted me to meet; male and female. People suggested that it would be good to meet "other women like me". I hated this idea. Just because another woman is going through a divorce, does not make us exactly the same. While reaching out to other women in a similar situation may be an effective coping tool for some, I knew that it wasn't for me. I didn't want to bond with someone over our shared heartache. Re-hashing my marriage and commiserating with other women wasn't a good option for me. I support the idea of support groups, but only for finding common ground in your efforts to move forward. I was worried about getting hung up on my past and therefore unable to forge a future filled with positive mental health, and happiness.

> **Dr. J Says:**
>
> Support groups are excellent for people who feel alone or isolated, who have few others to share with and who enjoy meeting others in a group setting. Very introverted or private people may find meeting people in a group setting daunting. Others may feel the negative experiences of others color their own. I encourage everyone to try a group out to see if it is for them. Online groups are also an option for those who find a group setting stressful.. Trying something new can sometimes be an eye opening, positive experience.

I certainly knew that my pending divorce would shape me and change me, but I was just as certain that I didn't want to be defined by it. I didn't want divorce to be my entire label. Divorce isn't who I am. It's something I'm going through. I wanted to keep those lines very clear. For me, this was fundamental in reconstructing my happiness.

I needed to be strong and emotional, and I needed to learn from my mistakes by accepting my past decisions. That's who I needed to be, and that's what I had to figure out how to do. I was standing in my present; Rocky, dirt road behind me, scattered with some mistakes and heartbreak, but not all bad. I needed to learn how to identify the cause of that rocky road so that I could pave a bright and smooth road ahead for me and my kids. All the tools were there. I just had to find them and figure out how to use them.

Getting involved in the dating scene would only have clouded my journey and compromised my main objectives. I needed to stay focused and heal before I could consider dating. How could I possibly know what type of man I wanted to be with, if I didn't even know me? I had to start with me.

I didn't go through this hell only to repeat my same mistakes.

I was going to re-build a stronger, healthier and better version of me. I owed it to myself and I certainly owed it to my kids.

It's not a bad thing to date right away. Many men and women need that self-esteem boost after a painful break up. I get it, but it's my firm opinion that this self-esteem boost needs to come from within you. Find what you need from your friends and create who you want to be from within yourself. It's only once you've done this that you are in a healthy headspace to know what you're looking for. Having said that however, each person needs to determine what they need and only you can say what's right for you. If dating is what you feel you need, then go for it. Just be sure to not allow dating to distract you from the task of rebuilding yourself.

Relying on dating as a way of boosting your self-esteem in my mind, is a backwards approach. I needed to build up my own sense of self-worth to be able to objectively and effectively date men who I believed were worthy of me! This was a huge ah-ha moment for me. And I was only able to reach this epiphany by taking time to rebuild myself. There was nothing more satisfying to me, than knowing that I improved me. It took a long time for me to date. I waited what didn't seem like a long time to me, but must have seemed like ages to all the curious and inquisitive people in my life.

The idea of dating was a really scary concept for me, and yet it's also the most asked about topic by my friends and even by my acquaintances. There seems to be a phenomenon whereby people, close friends and others, are particularly curious about your dating life. I'm not sure if they're just trying to make conversation, trying to live vicariously through my seemingly exciting life or whether they're just wishing me happiness and feel that dating will solidify that happiness. It's interesting to me, regardless of reason, that people's questions always include, "so, are you dating?"

All of a sudden, I was hearing things like, "you should meet X. He's recently divorced too. Very nice guy". Or "Do you know my friend Y, he's great. I should introduce you".

As well-intended as it was, I simply wasn't ready. The thought of it actually put me into a state of physical discomfort.

We all have our own timetable for when we're ready to start dating. There's no magic number of days or weeks or months, or even a set time period that we should wait. There's no prescribed set of rules. Do what feels right for you.

When my marriage ended I needed to take things day by day and really provide stability for me and for my kids. Dating was the absolute furthest thing from my mind. I couldn't let anyone in. I encased myself in a bubble and I feared that if anyone tried to get in, my bubble would burst and I would fall to pieces.

I was adamant that I needed to heal and rebuild my life before I was ready to even think about dating. How did I spend my time when my kids were with their dad? Figuring out finances, paying bills, watching TV, spending time with friends, crying. I was in no state of mind to be "putting myself out there".

I had my good friends, I needed to appreciate my alone time and I needed to get my bearings and catch my breath. The length of time it takes us to get there is a very personal and individual journey. There's no rush. Take your time. I was not interested in online dating. It works for most of my friends and I have no objection to it, as long as one is careful. Simply put, it just wasn't for me. I've always been a very private person (which is why this book will come as a shock to many who know me) and the thought of creating such a public profile and chatting with random seekers just wasn't the right fit for me. It didn't feel right.

When asked why I wasn't on these sites, my response was simple and honest, "Because any guy that I end up with is too busy with his kids to be on these sites". That's truly how I felt.

I completely understand the desire to be desired and how nice it is to receive some much overdue attention and affection. I don't discourage this method of finding love. I had been out with enough girlfriends who were glued to their smartphones responding to interested and seemingly interesting men to know that I didn't want to be consumed with that type of search. Not at this point in my life. I wanted to focus on what I had in my life. I had lost so much but I still had a lot too, and I needed desperately to make sure that what I had was still intact…my kids. Myself; my future self.

I believe that in order to meet the right person, you need to be in a good headspace. How could I have even known what to look for if I had no idea what I wanted? And how could I possibly know what I wanted when I was just getting to know me?

Like many women in my situation, I knew what I didn't want but that doesn't mean that we know what we want. I needed to heal. I needed to figure out who I was and only then, was I able to know and become my future self. And quite honestly, it wasn't until I had embraced being alone, and I knew myself that I was truly ready to take a leap of faith.

And a leap of faith, I took! I had become quite close with someone who I had known for several years. Over time we had become family friends, while we were both still married. He had separated quite a bit before I did, and even once separated, he and his children spent time with our family.

As it turned out, once I had separated, our weekend schedules of when we had our kids and when we didn't matched up. Spending time together when we were both missing our kids was a very natural way to pass the time. Eventually our friendship evolved into something more, but it didn't happen neatly or easily. He was so respectful of my need to wait and simply keep our friendship as it was. He gave me the space I needed.

There was never any pressure and there was never any awkwardness between us. He continued to date here and there, and while I found myself getting a little jealous over time, I was determined to not allow this to cloud my readiness meter.

I would date when I was ready. Not a moment sooner. When I finally did feel ready, I was scared. I hadn't dated anyone in close to 17 years, other than a casual coffee here and there, but I was finally ready to give it a shot. I'm so glad that I did. I started dating my best friend. In the beginning while our relationship was still evolving and still new, we had lots to figure out, but we've always been happy together. I'm happy. My kids needed stability, and so did I. We took things very slowly, even breaking up for a while because we didn't seem to be on the same page. We're back together now and stronger than ever. I'm in a good place. My ex seems happy in his relationship, and I know that I am truly happy in mine.

CHAPTER

21

The Next Chapter

"I cannot let anger and hurt be my engine. I need to move with the big picture always on my mind, and the kids first and foremost."

– Jennifer Garner

Where the next chapter takes me, I'm not sure. I do know however, that I will embrace it with my new found tools, and I will stay true to my new self, every step of the journey. I will continue to work towards my future self but I'm where I need to be. My future self from the beginning of this ride has become my new self. It will require tweaking, re-evaluating, transitioning and sometimes relapses to my old ways, but if I am able to keep perspective and catch myself, then I will be able to stay on track. Life's journey isn't smooth, nor is it one directional. There are turns and setbacks but part of being human is our ability to be resilient if we learn how. That's what this process is all about.

My separation and divorce was painful and gut-wrenching, but it was a necessary journey and looking back, I am glad that I met this journey with strength, perseverance, determination and class. I am stronger now for my journey and my children are happy and well adjusted. I am grateful for all that I have and I no longer mourn what I lost. Because in the end, once the dust settles you begin to pick up the pieces of your life, you only have to pick up the pieces you want to keep. The rest can get tossed out and replaced by stronger, more shatter-proof pieces. It's with these old and new pieces that you're able to reconstruct your happy. You rebuild yourself, your family and your life.

I wish you much success and happiness once you reach the next chapter on your journey to your revised "happily ever after". But for now, while you're in the painful part, I give you love, I offer you positive energy and I wish you strength to keep going. Pick up the pieces that you want. This is your chance to rebuild. You're a custom order...built as you wish. Good luck and G-d bless.

Section Five

The Business
of Divorce

Advice from Family Law experts and Financial Professionals

"Ah, yes, divorce…from the Latin word meaning to rip out a man's genitals through his wallet."

– Robin Williams

"How I Love Lucy was born? We decided that instead of divorce lawyers profiting from our mistakes, we'd profit from them. "

– Lucille Ball

It's now time to look at your divorce from another angle…strategy and negotiation. This is now a business relationship, and should be handled as such. I hated this process. Since I was married to a Divorce Lawyer for almost 1.5 decades, I had a lot more behind-the-scenes knowledge and understanding of how this process works albeit, I didn't have a thorough understanding until I was sitting at the negotiation table.

Your lawyer is a wonderful resource to have. He/she will provide you with knowledge and information regarding your rights and they will stand up to your spouse in ways that you wish you could. It's important however to remember who your lawyer is and what their role is in your divorce.

<u>Keep Your Eye on the Prize: Remember Your Long Term Goals</u>

Your marriage to the person across the table has ended but your relationship as Co-parents is just beginning. Conduct yourself accordingly. Remember that whatever legal decisions you make will have an impact on your kids even though they won't (or shouldn't) know the details. Make sure you know which points are important to you. What are you willing to give up? What are you willing to compromise on? Just as you need to parent for the long term well-being of your children, you need to negotiate in the same way. You should make your priorities known to your lawyer as well so that he/she can negotiate effectively on your behalf.

Remember also, that before you get caught up in a nickle-and-dime-game, you're both taking money out of your children's pockets and putting it into your lawyers'.

Keep it in perspective.

Finding the Right Lawyer

<u>Find a Specialist</u>

You need to hire a lawyer who specializes in Family Law. You wouldn't go to your Family Doctor when you need heart surgery; you would seek the expertise of a Cardiologist. This is no different. If you're unfamiliar with Family Law Lawyers, speak to friends or people you know who have gone through a divorce. Maybe they were happy with their lawyer, maybe they weren't. If they weren't happy with their lawyer, then find out who their spouse used. While there are likely many Family Law Lawyers in your area, they tend to be a tight community. Once you start asking questions, you're likely to hear many names and perhaps even hear the same names multiple times. Make a list of all names. It's a starting point from which to jump.

<u>Do Your Research</u>

Once you've put together a list of Lawyers, research them. Do a Google Search, browse their website and learn about them and their firm. Be careful however, when searching those "Rate Your Lawyer" types of sites. Look at how many reviews the person has received and always take this information with a grain of salt. Everyone's divorce is different, so this isn't always the best gauge.

Start to think about what you want and what your case needs. Do you prefer a male or female lawyer, or are you indifferent? Do you need an aggressive litigator or do you anticipate an amicable settlement? **In many cases, the lawyer that you choose will set the tone for your negotiations. Choose wisely and choose based on your circumstances.**

Does the lawyer have children? This may not matter, but perhaps you feel more comfortable that someone with kids will understand your childcare issues. Again, it has to do with your comfort level.

Do they have any specialties within Family Law? Do you require them to? For example, if you anticipate a nasty fight, you may wish to pair up with a lawyer who has litigation experience. If you have complicated financial statements or property issues, then you may want a lawyer who has experience with these issues. If you and/or your spouse own your own business, this may be helpful.

Personality is important too. Does your lawyer understand your objectives? In my case for example, I needed an aggressive lawyer because of my spouse's profession, but I also didn't anticipate a bitter war. I had to find a lawyer with a good balance; someone who wasn't afraid to go up against my ex and his lawyer, but someone who was reasonable and with an objective to settle amicably. I fired my first lawyer because he didn't seem on board with my objectives. He's a phenomenal lawyer with an incredibly good reputation, but he wasn't the right fit for my needs. My second lawyer fit the bill. Which brings me to the next important point…?

<u>Shop Around A Bit…</u>

Research and reputation are helpful, but you need to know how your lawyer will work for and with you. This is YOUR divorce and you need to be in control. Your lawyer is there to explain your rights to you, to advocate on your behalf, and offer objectivity where you aren't able to, but ultimately, you're in the driver's seat.

Meet with 3 or 4 lawyers. Many lawyers offer free initial consultations for this purpose. Talk to them and get a sense for who they are and what they can do for you. Do you connect with them? Do you feel comfortable with them? This is very important.

In meeting with a few lawyers for this book, they had some valuable advice for you when it comes to shopping around... Be skeptical of the lawyers who tell you that they can get you everything you want. Be careful of those who make you all sorts of promises. If they're telling you everything that you want to hear, it may be a sales pitch. Of course, this too depends on your circumstances and what you're looking to receive.

Geographic Desirability

Laws are specific to each jurisdiction and depending on where you live; your rights and entitlements may differ. You absolutely require a lawyer in your jurisdiction, who can advise you, but you also want to find a lawyer who is convenient for you. You may require several meetings with your lawyer during the course of negotiations, so make sure that you're comfortable with where they're located. My lawyer for example was downtown and in rush hour could take me over an hour to get to. We arranged meetings during non-rush hour times and we also arranged telephone meetings. Make sure that you're able to make arrangements to meet with your lawyer.

Trust

Just as you have to put your faith in your child's Pediatrician, you need to put your faith in your lawyer. Trust that they're acting in your best interests and allow them to do their job.

Communication

HEATHER TANNENBAUM

You need to be able to speak with your lawyer freely and he/she must be able to have a clear understanding of your objectives. If you're not sure of your objectives, your lawyer will help you to figure them out. This must be done early on in the process to provide your lawyer with an understanding of how to proceed with your case.

My objective for example, was to ensure that I received a fair deal. I was concerned that my ex and I were not on the same playing field, given his profession. I needed a lawyer who could pick out any and all points that were potentially unfair to me.

"If marriage is grand, then what's divorce? Answer: Ten grand."

– Unknown

Your Lawyer's Role

The list of criteria thus far, isn't much different than what you would look for in a spouse. That's because you will establish a relationship with your lawyer. Due to the nature of the lawyer/client relationship, you will (or you ought to) feel comfortable confiding in your lawyer about any and all matters pertaining to your marriage so that your lawyer can determine their relevance in your divorce.

Let's be clear however that your lawyer is neither your therapist nor your friend. Your lawyer's job is to act in your best interest and advise you on the best way to achieve your desired result. Your lawyer is there to ensure that your rights are protected and to get you the best possible legal outcome. It is so common for people to cry to their lawyers about how awful their spouse is. My ex would come home from the office so many times, telling me about such situations. Friendly words of advice...therapists are cheaper than lawyers!

How to Get the Most Bang for Your Buck

Be Efficient

Understand that your lawyer is billing you for his/her time, and you're billed for every minute, every letter, every email correspondence, and every phone call to you or your ex's lawyer. Your bills will add up quickly and it's so important to be mindful of this when you initiate this process. You definitely want your lawyer to invest time in understanding the particulars of your case, but be wise with how you use your lawyer and essentially how you spend your money.

Leave your emotions out of the meeting. It's tough. I'm guilty of this too; we all do it but be aware of it and try to conduct your meetings as though they're business meetings because that's exactly what they are. You've now entered the business of divorce and I urge you to govern yourself accordingly. Stick to facts; not feelings.

Be forthright with your lawyer and provide all pertinent information in a timely manner.

Do Your Homework

I knew and understood certain concepts, having been exposed to divorce language while I was married. Now that I was the one going through it however, I needed to understand things like child support, net family property, sole vs. joint custody and many other terms commonly used in family law. Instead of paying my lawyer to explain them to me, I did my own research. You've got a wealth of knowledge at your fingertips. A few internet searches and I was good to go.

Once I had a basic understanding, I was better prepared for my meetings and I was able to make more educated decisions quicker.

Some Google searches that I recommend you conduct prior to your first lawyer's meeting are as follows:

1. Common divorce terms
2. Divorce questions
3. Divorce preparation checklist

This is a good starting point, and you can always refine your search, based on what you learn from these primary searches. For example, if you're unclear on what a term means, you can always search up a clearer definition of the term.

Be sure however that when you're searching, you're using information that's relevant to your country, province, or state. This is very important.

Fun fact: the term "attorney" is only used in the United States.

Be Prepared

When meeting with your lawyer, make sure you've done any prep work. Read over materials and familiarize yourself with them prior to your meeting. Make notes and record questions so that when you're face to face with your lawyer, you're not wasting time. Be your own advocate. If you don't understand something, ask. If you aren't comfortable with a suggestion, speak up. This is YOUR divorce and you need to be satisfied with the result.

What to expect at your first meeting:

At the first meeting, you should leave with an opinion regarding your case. You should be given the basics of family law and what your rights and obligations are. Some general information should be provided and you should leave with an overview of your case.

You should be able to ask questions and don't be afraid to ask your lawyer some questions about them. For example:

Have you done a case like this before?

Who will be working on the file? Will it be primarily the lawyer, a clerk, an associate? And how will they bill you for this?

Also be aware that a lawyer should never charge you for research on your case that they should otherwise know. You can expect to be charged for their time to research if there are specific and uncommon details pertaining to your case specifically.

What's their policy on returning phone calls? How quickly can you expect a call to be returned? This is the biggest complaint among clients.

Ask what you're getting at the consultation; you should walk out with an opinion about your case and be weary of the lawyer who tells you everything you want to hear.

A Recommended List of "Don'ts" from the Family Law Experts:

DON'T make financial arrangements or significant purchases without notifying or consulting with your lawyer.

DON'T post things on social media that are inappropriate, or can damage your case in any way.

DON'T drain joint bank accounts or lines of credit.

DON'T speak to the children about inappropriate issues pertaining to legal proceedings.

DON'T refuse to provide the children to the other parent during his/her scheduled time with the children.

DON'T agree to any type of financial settlement without consulting your lawyer.

A lawyer's job is to educate the client on their case and how the issues of family law work in their case.

"A lawyer's job is to assist in and facilitate a settlement. The lawyer's job is to get the client what they want, but also be able to step back and advise you if you're being reasonable and acting in the best interests of the children and the family. The lawyer has an obligation to the client but also should feel an obligation to create as little trauma on the family as possible in seeking the desired results."

Getting Your Finances in Order

In the early days of separation, divorce or the contemplation of either, you're no doubt going to be concerned about your finances. Can you afford to divorce? Can your family financially manage 2 homes and are you going to be able to maintain your current lifestyle? Will you have to owe money to your former spouse or will they owe you? You're likely going to have many questions and if this process is as overwhelming to you as it was to me, here is some information that I gathered from a few Financial Planners to help guide you and hopefully help you generate a plan to be prepared and protected. I have spoken with two Canadian Financial Planners and an American Certified Divorce Financial Analyst, named Shawn Leamon. Shawn is an MBA and runs the most listened to PodCast on iTunes for managing your finances during the divorce process. You can access all of Shawn's podcasts at www.DivorceAndYourMoney.com

Wherever you live, there are some universal and basic questions that you need to ask yourself in order to financially prepare yourself for divorce:

1. Can You Save Your Marriage?

This is a very personal question with a very personal conclusion that only you can determine.

2. Do You Have Your Own Bank and Credit Accounts?

You need to set up accounts in your own name for general life purposes post-divorce, but also because as Leamon says, "joint assets have a tendency to disappear" during the divorce process. You're no longer making joint financial decisions and you therefore need to protect yourself and prepare to control your own money.

3. **Have You Checked Your Credit Report?**

Leamon says that this is an important step regardless of where you are in your divorce process. Go to credit bureaus (Equifax, TransUnion or any website that provides you with your free credit score). Equifax Canada and TransUnion Canada are two national credit bureaus available for Canadians. Learn about all accounts linked to your name. This includes credit cards, loans, lines of credit, car or furniture financing. If you've ever had a mortgage, bank loan, car loan, student loan and any money that you have ever borrowed will all show up on your credit report. You need to obtain this information for 2 reasons, according to Leamon.

a) to ensure that it's accurate
b) to ensure that there are no surprises

The credit report will tell you everything that you need to know so that you're able to know where you stand and to protect yourself as you embark upon this process.

4. How Will You Pay for Your Divorce?

Lawyers, financial experts, therapists, real estate appraisers, private investigators, certified business valuators all cost money and at least some of these will be required during your divorce. Leamon strongly suggests that you make sure that you have a method to pay for all of this. He says that you need a plan going into this process. Do you need to get a loan from a divorce funding company? Do you need to borrow money from family? Do you need to sell some of your assets (jewellery for example).

Leamon also suggests that you do the following 3 things:

1. **Create a budget:** Have a sense of your after tax income and all your expenses.

2. **Create a written agreement:** This refers to a legally binding agreement with respect to your finances. What you're responsible for, what your ex is responsible for. This needs to be in writing because you need recourse if he/she doesn't keep up their end of the deal. Also in the US, many states (though not all) recognize separation and therefore you require your lawyer to draft a separation agreement for you and your ex to both execute.

3. **Reduce expenses:** Leamon warns that you shouldn't expect to maintain your same lifestyle post-divorce. "When you're going from one household to two with the same income, things can get very expensive, very quickly", and you don't want to accumulate debt. He suggests figuring out what to cut by going through every dollar and determining whether you can cut it. Leamon says that even cutting $10/month can quickly add up to a significant savings.

All the professionals that I spoke to advise you to find out what's yours, and make copies. This includes:

- Income tax returns and any amendments
- (In the US this would include any W-2 forms, 1099 forms, K-1 forms)
- Pre-nuptial agreements
- Bank statements
- Investment account statements
- Loan & mortgage statements

- Retirement savings accounts
- (In the US this would include IRA, SEP-IRA, ROTH IRA, 401K, 403B)
- Children's bank accounts (In the US includes 529)
- Children's documents (birth certificates, SIN (Canada) Social Security Numbers (US)
- Wills
- Power of Attorney documents
- Bank & investment accounts

  (outside of registered accounts such as RRSPs and TFSAs in Canada), mortgages and credit cards can be jointly-held, meaning at the time of their opening you and your partner agreed to have joint access to the money. (This is a common arrangement for spouses as it avoids unnecessary legal costs and delays at death.) Our Canadian experts suggest that you consider freezing or cancelling any joint credit cards. Notify any lenders where you have jointly borrowed money that you want to change the terms of the arrangements so that the approval of both spouses is required to borrow additional monies or alter the debts. Once that is done, the couple can work on figuring out how the joint debts will be handled as part of the settlement of assets pursuant to the divorce proceedings.

Some other actions to take include the following:

1. **Change your online passwords — and don't forget about telephone access**

This is good practice at the best of times, but especially so during periods of vulnerability. Even if you were the primary financial caretaker, your spouse likely knows your commonly used user names and passwords. If you're unsure of how to access your own documents, call the respective custodians to change your online and telephone access.

2. Get your tax returns and all supporting documents

If your partner handled your tax filings, ask for your supporting documents and files. In Canada, documents that support your annual tax filings can be requested of you by the CRA up to 7 years after their filing. If the filings were handled by a professional, ensure information is released only to you.

For Canadians, you can create and access your tax profile online via the CRA's website. This is an invaluable resource at any stage in life, but all the more so if you're trying to understand your finances for the first time.

3. Update your beneficiaries

Most have named their former partner as the beneficiary of their registered accounts (in Canada, RRSPs,TFSAs, RIFs, LIRAs, etc.) Be sure to update your beneficiaries to another loved one or your estate (meaning everything reverts to the instructions in your will). Custodians usually have a simple one-page form letter available online.

4. Update your will

It would be a shame to have the dust settle on your divorce, acrimonious or not, and then have your rightful heirs have to battle your ex on the distribution of your estate. Your divorce doesn't have to finalize before tackling this item.

5. Benefits

If you were covered under your spouse's health and travel benefits plan, your coverage may be void upon separation and/or divorce. Be aware of your exposure; an accident abroad can be a financially devastating event if you've previously never had to consider buying travel insurance. Previously covered healthcare expenses like teeth cleanings and chiropractic appointments are expensive when paid out-of-pocket.

6. Talk to the people you know are in charge

Your bankers, money managers and accountants all have a fiduciary duty to act in your best interest and keep your information confidential. Update them all about your situation. If necessary, update or revoke Power of Attorney documents.

7. Ask for help

Your support group is your best resource for financial referrals. Ask who your friends and family use as their portfolio managers, accountants or debt counsellors.

Our financial experts warn us too, that your lawyer is not your grief counsellor, financial advisor, accountant or, in many cases, even your friend. They are also likely to be the most expensive professional service you are to engage. You're encouraged to keep your communication with your lawyer professional and succinct. Stay organized.

Tips for investing in your kids' future

In Canada, there are two common ways of saving for your kids' futures. Most parents (and grandparents) opt for the registered education savings plan (RESP) to save for future education expense. With this, contributions made are topped-up by the government for use toward future post-secondary tuition. The mandate of this type of savings plan is exclusively geared toward future education costs. The account is held in the parent or grandparent's name, but withdrawals can only be made by showing proof of the child's enrolment in a post-secondary institution.

Secondly, parents may open informal trust (ITF) accounts (emphasis on 'informal') for minors. For example, Jane Smith can open a 'Jane Smith ITF Junior Smith' investment account. There are a couple ways to set it up, but effectively at age 18 Junior has legal access to the funds. ITF accounts are a popular way to save and account for money meant for a specific child.

Higher net worth families can also explore formal trusts, where the assets are held in a trust account and may only be disbursed according the rules outlined in the trust document.

Any financial planner or Certified Divorce Financial Analyst would be able to help you set up whatever you need. I would encourage you to speak to a professional so that you're able to take advantage of all options available to you, given your specific circumstances.

CPSIA information can be obtained
at www.ICGtesting.com
Printed in the USA
LVHW04s2023241018
594711LV00002B/3/P